FROM BLOODY
HERRLISHEIM
TO A
SLAVE LABOR CAMP

JAMES E. MUSCHELL

James E. Muschell

United Associates
Cheboygan, Michigan

Published by United Associates
111 North Main Street
Cheboygan, MI 49721

Publisher's Cataloging-in-Publication Data
Muschell, James E.

From bloody Herrlisheim to a slave labor camp / by James E. Muschell.
– Cheboygan, MI : United Associates, 2005.

p. ; cm.
ISBN: 0-9770648-0-8
ISBN13: 978-0-9770648-0-9

1. World War, 1939-1945—Prisoners and prisons, German. 2. World War, 1939-1945—Personal narratives, American. 3.Prisoners of war—United States. 4. Prisoners of war—Germany. I. Title.

D805.G3 M87 2005
940.54/7243/092—dc22   2005906604

Book production and coordination by Jenkins Group, Inc.
www.bookpublishing.com
Interior design by Chad Miller
Cover design by Jamie E. Muschell

Printed in the United States of America
09 08 07 06 05 • 5 4 3 2 1

Contents

Prologue

It has been more than 60 years since I was subjected to some of the ravages of the Nazi regime as a *kriegsgefangene*, the German word for prisoner of war. The years have slipped by, but my memory is still intact, and there aren't too many of us left who were involved in the final serious German offensive termed Nordwind that became known as the "Second Battle of the Bulge," or the "Little Bulge." In that battle, our 43rd Tank Battalion was wiped out and our division, the 12th Armored, lost 1,249 men killed or captured during the month of January, 1945. This was one of the least known campaigns and a secret kept by the American Command until a few years ago when information became available under the Freedom of Information Act.[1]

A *second* Battle of the Bulge? That's exactly what it was, but in this case the German offensive was successful and resulted in a significant German breakthrough. Had this been commonly known among the American forces, its demoralizing and possibly devastating effect would certainly have traveled up and down the American lines and those of our allies. Hence, in hindsight, it was easily understood why it went reported only to those in top-level command status and on a close hold "need-to-know" basis.

I was wounded and captured in this battle in Alsace Lorraine, France. As a young, naïve American soldier, I did not expect nor did I have any reason to believe that a civilized society, even under the Nazi government, could be guilty of such brutality and still maintain the support of the German people. Now I believe that, with very few exceptions, the German people did know what was going on in the concentration camps and in the death and slave labor camps. The accompanying smoke from the incineration of bodies, particularly from the large chimneystacks, had a very pungent odor recognizable as the smell of death.

In a very short time, as a detached prisoner of war (POW) of the Nazis, I realized they were capable of de-humanizing people with unspeakable acts of brutality, including starvation, working prisoners to death, and outright murder, later judged as Crimes against Humanity, which incidentally was count four of the indictment of the Nazi defendants at the Nuremberg trials.[2] (A detached prisoner of war was a prisoner of war who was transferred from a Geneva Convention-recognized prisoner of war *stalag* [camp] to a slave labor camp.)

As an American detached prisoner of war, I believed we were fighting for a democratic country whose principles were based on a free society. My beliefs were the same as my dad's, who was wounded and gassed in France while fighting the Germans in World I. We were simply there doing our jobs without a lot of patriotic hoopla, knowing that in the interests of human decency it was our duty as soldiers to defeat a fascist government headed by a dictator who was attempting world domination and the enslavement of free people and the pogrom known as the "Final Solution" by exterminating the Jewish people in gas chambers and enslaving and exterminating other Nazi-defined *untermenschens* (sub-humans), including Gypsies, Russians, Poles, and yes, even some Americans. Six million Jewish people were murdered; today's expression for such mass murder is ethnic cleansing. The Nazi's main objective regarding us POWs was to starve us to death or work us to death.

Years have passed, and though I am no longer re-living the daily horror of being a prisoner of war, I still have many painful memories. Although most of our small group of Americans in the detached slave labor camp were not of Jewish extraction, we were considered inferior and sub-human by those bastards the SS (short for Schutzstaffel, Hitler's protective police squadrons), who were the power behind the commandants in charge of the prisoner of war camps, the slave labor detachments, and all of the death camps, concentration camps, and execution squads. Since I had lost my dog tags, they perhaps thought I was Jewish and had purposely thrown them away. (If I had been Jewish, my dog tags would have been marked with an "H," indicating that I was of Hebrew extraction.)

The purpose of this writing is to create a memorial to my companions who died at "Bloody Herrlisheim" in Alsace Lorraine, France, and to those in our slave labor camp who became my friends, as well as to all of the Jewish, Polish, and Russian prisoners who died in the concentration and prisoner of war camps, as well as to those who suffered inhumane treatment, starvation, bombing, and strafing and survived. For those who are unable to speak or write about their experiences for themselves, I write this as a record of what happened to many persons of several nationalities during World War II.

This writing and my personal experience are also a reminder of what can happen when a society loses a free press, becomes too passive or indifferent to excessive propaganda by unscrupulous politicians, and when its citizens fail to exercise their privilege of voting in a democratic society. Such was the case in Germany, which allowed Hitler and his followers to take control of the country. As a world power and a free nation, in conjunction with the United Nations, America cannot let this happen again anywhere in the world.

Alarmingly, in spite of the facts, the seeds of revisionism are being sown today by various groups and individuals who would have us believe that the Holocaust and the ethnic cleansing of Jews, Russians, and Poles and the brutal treatment of prisoners of war and forced slave laborers that took place in Europe during World War II was merely wartime propaganda. Thus, it is also my hope that this writing will in some small way help silence those so-called historians who are attempting to revise history by denying that the Holocaust and related acts of genocide occurred.

Likewise, I am at times still filled with despair and disgust because there is very little factual information in our present day school history books relating to the Holocaust and the Nazi's plan for working and starving to death other prisoners of war and Nazi-designated *untermenschens*. There seems to be a growing movement towards total denial that this, too, ever happened.

My official designated prisoner of war camp was Stalag X1 B in Fallingbostel, Germany, where I was issued a wooden dog tag (the term "dog tag" was used by the U.S. Army) containing my German identification number, 135085. I, along with a very small group of Americans, was almost immediately transferred to a slave labor detachment in the city of Hannover, Germany, consisting of Poles, Russians, and Jews from the nearby death camp Bergen Belsen. I have no idea why we Americans were selected for the slave labor detachment, as opposed to a prisoner of war camp, because none of us to my knowledge were Jewish, but we may have been considered misfits. Some of the prisoners were checked to see if they had been circumcised. I was not checked.

In compliance with German Order Number 75 regarding prisoners of war, we were kept separated at night, in different camp buildings, from prisoners who spoke languages other than English. However, we all worked together in a petroleum refining and fuel storage tank facility during the daytime and we were often sent into the city of Hannover to clean up after Allied bombings, though this violated Section 743 of Germany's prisoner of war regulations (See Appendix E).[3] Like many of the terms of the Geneva Convention, this was agreed to by Germany but ignored in particular by the SS. While working in Hannover, I met an American civilian who was caught by the war as an American employee of the refining facility. Originally from Brooklyn, New York, he never did give us his name, although he spoke with an American accent.

The treatment and brutality we endured and the suffering we experienced is still deeply imbedded in my mind, and I am able to recall in detail some of the horrors I witnessed as a prisoner of war. For those who deny that the Holocaust ever happened, I have a series of original pictures taken at a German prison camp at Landsburg, Germany, that substantiate the Nazi terror. These were taken by Robert J. Hartwig, C Company, 134th Ordinance Battalion, of our 12th Armored Division that liberated the camp. The Landsburg jail, incidentally, is where Hitler wrote *Mein Kampf*.

Not all the prisoner of war camps were the same, nor were they as brutal as the detached slave labor camps, many of which were not identified and did not have written records. According to the U.S. Military Archives Department, "After December 1944, the Germans destroyed most of their records." There hasn't been very much written about these groups or about the 78,000 Allied soldiers still missing and unaccounted for from World War II in the European Theater of Operations.[5]

Those 78,000 Allied soldiers were either executed, starved to death, died from disease, or were strafed by friendly fire or bombed, because most of the detached camps for prisoners of war and slave labor personnel were not identified as such and the Allies had no way of knowing who they were bombing. As Section 848 of German Orders states, "Prisoner of war camps in the home war zone are not to be made recognizable for enemy air forces." Those deaths that resulted undoubtedly went unreported, in spite of German Order Number 23, issued at the beginning of the war for prisoners of war (See Appendix E).

I was also advised by a Polish fellow slave laborer, Bejec Woichevski,[6] that a number of Allied soldiers who had escaped from German camps and headed east were taken prisoner by the Russians near the end of the war in camps near the Eastern Sector. Many of these prisoners, instead of being released and returned to American forces, may have been held as Russian prisoners or summarily executed.

Bejec, a Polish soldier who had been captured in 1939 during the invasion of Poland, had contact with the Polish underground via forced civilian slave laborers while a prisoner of the Germans. He advised us that if we were able to escape, we should head west, not east, because the Russians did not always distinguish between the Allies and the Germans when it came to taking prisoners of war. Knowing the terrible price in human life that the Russians suffered from the Nazis' invasion of Russia, I can understand their suspicion of anyone who was without proper identification papers.

Bejec also warned us that his contacts in the underground had informed him that since the war was going badly for Germany in early 1945 and the end was near, SS Reichsfuhrer Heinrich Himmler had ordered that no detached prisoners of war outside the designated *stalags* were to be liberated by the Allies. As a result, the Waffen SS, those members of the SS who had the power to execute on the spot all those who did not have proper papers or proper identification, had killing squads out looking for those who fit that description. Fortunately, a number of German officers and camp commandants knew that Germany was losing the war and ignored the order. Such an order was also given by Hitler after the fire bombing of Dresden on February 13, 1945, to kill all Allied prisoners of war. Thank God, a number of camp commandants ignored that order as well.

A written notice "To All Prisoners of War!" outlining some of the specifics pertaining to potential escaping prisoners of war is written as issued and can be found in Appendix C. Subsequent to this order, Carl J. Burchardt, president of the International Committee of the Red Cross in Geneva, Switzerland, reported that Adolf Hitler late in March of 1945 gave orders to also execute all American and British airmen captive in Germany.

Bejec Woichevski's contacts also reported that Hitler had ordered that Jewish- American prisoners of war were to be segregated and made part of the "Final Solution." This was confirmed by Lieutenant Col. M. Mark, U.S.A.F., of Forest Hills, New York.[7]

Another confirmation came from Bernie Melnick of Cape Coral, Florida. Melnick was a survivor of Berga, a slave labor camp approximately 114 kilometers (km.) or 70 miles southwest of Dresden near the Czech border. Melnick, like a number of other American prisoners of war, did not want to be accused of making up wild tales about being sent to a concentration camp. He also stated that "along with the Jewish soldiers were other GI Americans who were considered undesirable." He added, "The Americans also worked alongside religious and political prisoners from eastern European countries, such as Poland, and Hungary."[8]

Gerald Daub of the 100th Infantry Division was captured and imprisoned at Bad Orb Stalag 98 near Frankfort, Germany, and shortly thereafter was culled out with about 350 Americans who were identified as Jews, misfits, or those having Jewish features or who had been circumcised. He was transported to Berga, a satellite of Buchenwald in eastern Germany, and also became a slave laborer.[9]

Alfred Feldman, a survivor of Berga, said he gave a deposition about his ordeal to military war-crimes investigators after the war. That agency, like all others dealing with military matters, has no information about American POWs being in Berga.[10]

This is perhaps similar to my own experiences. After being liberated by the 15th Scottish Division near Celle, Germany, on April 13, 1945, I was turned over to American rehabilitation units. As part of my rehabilitation, I was ordered to sign a paper stating that I would not publish anything relating to the slave labor camp or what went on during my captivity for at least 10 years after the war was over. On that basis, this publication is somewhat behind schedule.

James E. Muschell, 2005
Corporal, Company B
43rd Tank Battalion
12th Armored Division

Introduction

By December of 1944, the Allied Forces on the Western Front had carried their offensive from the Normandy beaches to the gates of Germany. Enemy resistance stiffened as the Allies reached the German border. The problem of supplying the present total of 48 divisions in the European Theater of Operations was a major factor because the Allies had outrun their supplies. Since gasoline was limited and was of major concern for the armored forces, the general plan was to stockpile fuel depots, consolidate supply lines, and prepare for a spring offensive.

On December 16, 1944, the Germans under the command of General Gerd von Rundstedt launched an operation called Wacht am Rhein ("Watch on the Rhine"). This name was designed to provide a defensive rather than an offensive connotation. Hitler changed the code name "Wacht am Rhein" to "Autumn Mist" before attacking the unsuspecting Allied forces in the Ardennes.

The Allied defense in the Ardennes consisted of six divisions containing 83,000 men, while the Germans attacked with three armies, the 5th commanded by General von Manteuffel, the 7th commanded by General Erich Brandenberger, and the 6th Panzer Division ("*panzer*" is the German word for "tank") commanded by the notorious Sepp Dietrich, consisting of some 200,000 German soldiers.[11,12] Soon enough, this battle became known as the "Battle of the Bulge."

Hitler's plan was to capture the Port of Antwerp, a principal port supplying the Allied European forces, and to split the British and Canadian armies from the Americans and force a negotiated peace on the Western Front. Hitler was under the impression that a negotiated peace was possible with the Western Allies and would enable the Wehrmacht (German Regular Army) to move eastward the three armies along the Western Front in a last-ditch effort to stop the advancing Russians and drive them back to the east.

This was a desperate plan involving German troops dressed as Americans who created all sorts of confusion and dismay by misdirecting convoys and troop movements and changing directional traffic signs. As one account puts it, "Even who the enemy were was in doubt, for the treacherous Krauts were found to be using American tanks as well as dressing in American and British uniforms."[13]

 Operation Nordwind was launched at 23:00 on December 31, 1944, and was tied up with Field Marshal Gerd von Rundstedt's offensive in the Ardennes. The purpose of Operation Nordwind was not only to relieve the pressure in the Ardennes but also to recapture Strasbourg and move through the Saverne Gap. Himmler had promised Adolph Hitler he would recapture Strasbourg on the anniversary of the twelfth year of Hitler's rise to power. Strasbourg, the largest city and capital of the Alsace region, was a key strategic point.

When the Ardennes offensive began to fail, Adolph Hitler's strategy was to have von Rundstedt launch an attack through the lower Vosges Mountains and force a breakthrough in order to relieve the pressure being exerted upon the German troops in the Ardennes. (The Vosges are the mountains in northeast France on the west side of the

Rhine Valley.) Von Rundstedt withdrew some of his best troops, hastily re-equipped and re-manned them, and sent them to a small bridgehead the Germans had established in a sector between Strasbourg and the Maginot Line, centering in the villages of Herrlisheim and Gambsheim in the Alsace Lorraine region.

Involved in disputes for hundreds of years, this region was initially part of France and was forcefully annexed by Germany, which accounts for the German names of the cities and towns in the area. After World War I, as part of the 1918 treaty, it was returned to France; both German and French are still spoken there today.

Northwest of Herrlisheim, the German 6th SS-Mountain Division and the 256th Volks Grenadier Division captured the town of Wingen in the Vosges Mountains. The 361st Volks Grenadier Division succeeded in capturing Baerenthal in the Zintsel Valley.[14] The Germans also succeeded in driving a wedge between General Alexander Patch's VI and XV Corps.[15] On December 5, the 12th Armored Division was officially assigned to XV Corps.

Operation Nordwind began with Tiger tanks, well known as the best tanks of World War II. The Germans also used Tiger tanks for their frontal assault in Alsace Lorraine.[16] Unfortunately, the American tanks were 75 millimeter (mm.) or 76 mm. M4A3 medium tank guns and were no match for the Tiger tanks. Any time an American tank had a frontal attack or defensive action with a Tiger tank, the American tank was outgunned and destroyed. The only way an American tank could destroy a Tiger tank was by firing into the side or undercarriage.

The month of January, 1945, was the bloodiest chapter in the entire career of the 12th Armored Division, lasting from January 8 to 20. The Germans crossed the Rhine during the nights of January 5 and 6 and quietly established a bridgehead at Gambsheim and Herrlisheim with an offensive force consisting of the 553rd Volksgrenadier and the 405th Infantry Divisions, the SS Panzer Grenadier Division ("Liebestandarte Adolph Hitler"), the 17th SS Panzer Grenadiers, the 31st Panzer Division, and the 10th SS Panzer Grenadier Division. The plan was to break through the right flank of General Alexander Patch's 7th Army, which occupied an 84-mile thinly held line.

CHAPTER 1

Breaching the Maginot Line

The 12th Armored Division was originally activated in September of 1942. Nicknamed the "Hellcats," it began its crusade in Europe, assembling at Auffay, France, after crossing the English Channel. The division was originally assigned to the 9th Army, commanded by Lt. General William H. Simpson, and later reassigned to the 7th Army, commanded by Lt. General Alexander Patch. The division was also temporarily assigned to the 3rd Army, commanded by General George S. Patton, and the French 1st Army, commanded by d'Armee de Lattre de Tassigny. The 12th Armored Division was singled out for commendation from every corps under which it operated, VI, XV, XX, XXI, and the II French Corps.[17]

On May 5, 1945, at about 2:30 p.m., General Jacob Devers, General Alexander Patch, and General John O'Daniel of the 3rd

Infantry met with Field Marshal Albert Kesselring's staff to sign an unconditional surrender of all German forces in the region, including the German 19th Army. At 6:00 p.m. the same day, British General Bernard Montgomery met with a delegation from Germany and the successor of the dead Hitler, Admiral Karl Doenitz, who surrendered Germany unconditionally.[18]

For some reason the achievements of the 7th Army always received "second billing," either because of a lack of publicity or because other events took center stage. Neither General Jacob Devers nor General Alexander Patch sought publicity for themselves, and the general public may simply have been unaware of the accomplishments of the 7th Army from August 15, 1944, through May 8, 1945, though the men and officers who served in the 7th Army were very much aware of the effort and sacrifices. During this period, the 7th Army suffered 83,507 casualties in men killed, wounded, captured, or missing in action.[19]

On May 8, 1945, General Alexander Patch issued an order of the day expressing his assessment of the 7th Army. It states, "I have just received the following cable from the Secretary of War: 'I join a grateful nation in applauding the heroic part you and your men have taken in our triumph. Each soldier of the 7th Army shares in congratulations for the success gained through magnificent courage at the front. You can be proud of a distinguished accomplishment.[20]

This part of the 43rd Tank Battalion's history covers primarily the month of December 1944 and Germany's Operation Nordwind. Although Nordwind was not conducted on a scale comparable to that of Wacht am Rhein, its strategic objective was nearly as grand: it was intended to split the major subordinate elements of General Devers' 6th Army Group internally, along national lines. By separating the U.S. 7th Army from the French First Army, Hitler hoped to not only destroy the isolated American units in the Low Vosges and on the Alsatian Plain but to wreak decisive discord on the already strained relationship between U.S. President Franklin Roosevelt and French General Charles DeGaulle.[21]

As mentioned earlier, this was one of the least known campaigns and a secret kept for many years after the war. My battalion, the 43rd Tank Battalion, was wiped out on January 17, 1945, in a bloody battle in the town of Herrlisheim, Alsace Lorraine, France, where I was taken prisoner.

By the war's end, one thousand battle decorations had been awarded to the men of the division. One soldier was awarded the Congressional Medal of Honor 52 years after the war ended. This medal was presented posthumously at a ceremony in the White House by President Bill Clinton in 1997 to the family of Sergeant Edward A. Carter of D Company of the 56th Armored Infantry Battalion. Nine soldiers of the 12th Armored Division received the Distinguished Service Cross.[22]

The 12th Armored Division secretly relieved the 4th Armored Division at 06:00 on December 8, 1944. The 4th Armored Division was pulled back from the heavy fighting after it reached the Maginot Line to refit and rest. At the time we relieved the 4th Armored Division, they had no idea nor did we of what was to begin happening in the Ardennes on December 16, 1944, with the onslaught of Wacht am Rhein. On December 22, 1944, the 4th Armored Division began its drive north to relieve Bastogne. Patton moved three of his divisions, the 4th Armored, the 26th, and the 80th Infantry divisions, to relieve Bastogne within 72 hours. This was an extraordinary achievement in itself and was without a doubt a surprise to the Germans.

When we relieved the 4th Armored Division, they had already launched an attack on the town of Singling in the Maginot Line. We occupied the town of Singling on December 9, 1944. When we moved into Singling, we did so with considerable optimism because although our officers were supposed to know better, our tanks were bunched up in a haphazard fashion and could have offered an opportunity to the Germans had they known the situation. However, our tank crew was able to spend the night without being attacked, in an abandoned, quaint French home with beautiful, fine, finished furniture and rugs on the floors. The house even had a four-poster bed, and it was a welcome change for our crew to sleep inside a building instead of in the snow or a foxhole or sitting in our tanks with our bed roles wrapped around us. Our tank crew consisted of five men, and since only two could sleep in the bed, we flipped a coin to see who was chosen. I wasn't one of the lucky ones, but it was wonderful just to be able to sleep indoors. The weather was getting colder and conditions were chilly, wet, and miserable, so it was a primary concern to stay warm and dry.

On the morning of December 10, our tank took up a position on the high ground beyond the town. While holding the high ground beyond Singling, the first tank of Company B to be hit by anti-tank fire was commanded by Sergeant Kenneth Warner. One round struck the side of the tank before glancing off. Amazingly, although there was no significant damage, the shell grooved the steel armor plate much like a machine shop shaper would have done, creating a completely smooth gouge in the tank. Besides this, there was little opposition, so we completed the attack and occupied the town with only minor casualties.

Although the village of Singling was actually in the Maginot Line like a number of other villages, the fortifications of the Maginot Line were so constructed that the gun turrets swung in a complete circle. The exposed sides were defended by machine gun emplacements that could destroy small squads of infantry or tanks using machine guns or infantry shoulder-held *panzerfausts*. (This is the German term for "tank fist"; we call such a gun a bazooka.)

On December 11 we attacked the town of Guising. During this attack, I was operating a 30-caliber machine gun in the bow of the tank when a single German soldier with a *panzerfaust* stood up from a machine gun emplacement surrounded by sand-filled bags directly in front of our tank. He aimed directly at our tank, fired, and the shell glanced off the edge of our tank. A *panzerfaust* can knock out a tank, especially one of our Sherman tanks, with a direct hit on the carriage or through the steel plate at the bottom of the tank. Luckily, this did not happen. This soldier was not in a foxhole and was protected only by the sandbags, and I was able to keep him down behind the sandbags and interrupt his aim by firing repeated bursts from my machine gun in the bow of our tank so that before he could properly re-load and fire again, we ran over him. To this day, I can still remember his screams as he was ground underneath the tank tracks. He paid the price for not having dug a foxhole and for reyling on protection from the sandbags. In a foxhole, a soldier is protected because the tank can usually pass over the hole without killing the soldier. This is part of the basic training a soldier receives. It is much easier and cleaner to kill the enemy with a rifle or machine gun fire and with much less suffering than by grinding him up in the tank tracks.

War is hell, and as usual in combat, we had no choice but to kill or be killed. As mankind has been saying for hundreds of years, "No one in a civilized society should have to suffer such ravages of war." Other than this incident there was little resistance, and our tank column went right on through the town and continued on towards Bettviller. Our command post moved to Domfessel and prepared to attack on Corps orders the Maginot Line and to continue advancing to the Siegfried Line. (The Siegfried Line was the so-called West Wall behind the Franco-German border built by Hitler to offset any attack by the French from their Maginot Line.)

The Siegfried Line consisted of a veritable forest of concrete abutments in a series of triangular lines so that tanks could not advance in a straight direction. It appeared to me while walking through the Siegfried Line as a prisoner of war that by causing the tank to change direction between the concrete dragon's teeth while trying to advance, a tank would be exposing its sides and would be more vulnerable to anti-tank gun fire and would also be slowed down enough to be an easy target for the Germans' 88 mm. guns. (These guns, initially used as anti-aircraft guns, were also used on their Tiger tanks. General Erwin Rommel, commander of the Afrika Corps, was the first to use them as direct fire anti-tank guns.) The concrete abutments known as dragon's teeth were a bitch, but their concept did not consider American ingenuity.

I learned later that the Germans had not counted on the fact that the Americans, if unable to go straight through the wall with tanks, would go up and over, which they subsequently did by the use of bulldozers pushing earth masses in front to fill the voids and create a roadway up and over as a earthen bridge. The crossings were of course preceded by artillery and aircraft to knock out or eliminate the 88 mm. guns.

One of our first objectives was to breach the Maginot Line, and our tanks of the 43rd Battalion pulled up to where we could visibly observe the line and make a direct assault on the pillboxes. (Pillboxes were concrete circular or rectangular structures with protected entrances and gun ports that could fire 88 mm. guns directly at any advancing troops. The pillboxes were originally built by the French as part of the Maginot Line and were now being used by the Germans during their retreat).

The German 88 mm. gun was probably the best gun developed during World War II. It had such a high muzzle velocity that when pitted against our M4 Sherman tanks with 75 or 76 mm. guns, we generally didn't have a chance. Though we had high speed and power traverse for our gun turrets and the German Tiger tank turrets traversed much slower because they were hand traversed, this made little difference unless we could, because of our greater traverse speed and tank speed, get out of their way and out of their fire range before they could get us in their gun sights. When one of our tanks was hit with an 88 mm. shell, it generally went right through our armor, which I can personally attest to, not only because they used armor piercing shells but also because of the high muzzle velocity of the German 88 mm. gun, which was close to being comparable to a regular army rifle.

Our 75 mm. and the later-issued tanks with higher muzzle velocity 76 mm. tank shells generally did little or no damage when striking a Tiger tank unless we frightened them enough to withdraw or could fire at their less protected undercarriage. The Germans sometimes became frightened because the 7th and 3rd Army did have 90 mm. anti-tank guns in some areas of the front line, although in our area I did not see any such weapons available to us. Consequently, although the Germans had superior tanks, I believe they were uncertain at times as to whether or not we had newly modified or improved tanks. Unfortunately for us, the M26 medium tank with a 90 mm. gun was not introduced until early 1945, and to my knowledge not in our area.

On more than one occasion, we fired several consecutive 75 mm. rounds directly at the front of the Tiger tanks, and consistently each time the shell would glance off their armor without penetrating it. Believe me, this resulted in a sick feeling in the stomach, and all this time they would slowly be hand traversing their gun turret barrel towards your tank for a direct line of fire. Generally when they fired one 88 mm. round, you were hit, it was all over, and your tank was on fire or exploding. The crew was lucky if anyone survived. During my period of fighting up until I was captured, I was fortunate enough to survive five different tanks that were either destroyed, set on fire, or disabled by German tanks, *panzerfausts*, or anti-tank mines one way or another. As a result, I was able to serve under several different tank commanders.

While attempting to breach the Maginot Line as ordered, we began receiving artillery fire and direct fire from 88 mm. guns so we pulled our tanks to the back slope of a hill so the Germans could not see us directly. We then started to fire indirectly, using a forward observer. Our fire was so intense and heavy that our forward observer reported that the Germans were waving a white flag. We stopped firing and permitted a German officer to come forward. He spoke excellent English and stated that he wanted to talk with our commander about the terms for their surrender. He was asked to come closer with his hands in the air and he did so, coming up to the top of the rise so that he and our commanding officer could discuss the terms of the surrender.

This gave the German officer the opportunity of observing the general position of our tanks arranged for indirect fire. "Indirect fire" means firing tank guns without direct visibility guided by the directions given by radio from a forward observer. The forward observer could see where or what our shells were hitting and could then direct the gunners accordingly. Our commanding officer told the German officer they could surrender immediately and to leave all their weapons and come out in single file with their hands in the air. The German officer agreed and said he would go back and get the rest of the troops and would bring them up as stipulated and turn them over to us.

He was given permission to return so that he could get the rest of his troops. What followed was an example of Nazi fanaticism, because instead of returning and surrendering his troops, we were almost immediately subjected to a terrible barrage of artillery and mortar fire. It became apparent that the officer's sole purpose had been to see how our tanks were deployed on the back slope so as to be able to open fire with heavy artillery and mortars. As a result, another one of our tanks was hit on the side directly above the track, but it did not penetrate because it was a glancing hit and did not affect the tank's ability to continue the attack.

This whole act of treachery got everybody so dammed mad that our commanding officer decided to pull the tanks up to the top of the rise and take the risk of a direct hit so that we could concentrate our fire directly on the bastards. We did so, firing directly at the openings of the pillboxes and the gun ports. Because of the distance, we could not tell whether we made any direct hits on the gun ports. The pillbox entrances were generally offset with a heavy concrete wall directly inside the entrance opening. Further access to the inside area was at 90 degrees to the opening so that the soldiers would not be directly exposed to gunfire except through the gun port openings. Nonetheless, we put enough fire power and exploding shells into the entrance openings and towards the gun ports so that those who weren't killed by exploding shells or deafened by the concentrated noise inside the pillboxes reached a point where they decided to surrender for real, and they did. Afterwards, their enlisted men told me they'd wanted to surrender in the first place, but their officer was a Nazi fanatic party member and wouldn't do it.

We did not take any bullshit from any of them as we sent them back under guard. I rather suspect they were limited on the amount of ammunition they could fire at us, even though we were in an exposed position. The Germans were having supply difficulties, and our air force was continually strafing all roads and railways. After they surrendered and were sent back, we occupied the pillboxes that night. We were also able to make hot coffee and warm up our C-Rations. These were so named, I believe, because they were mostly canned foods. We had each been issued a small flexible can opener that we could carry with our dog tags, and believe it or not, these worked really well. During this period of December 8, 9, and 10, our division battle casualty reports consisted of 6 officers and 37 enlisted men killed, and 16 officers and 141 enlisted men wounded.

Our division's actions during December were divided into two phases. The first fighting took place from December 7 to 15 when we were opposed by elements of the 111th Panzer Division, which was fighting a delaying action supported by artillery from the Fortress of Bitche to the east and long-range railway artillery in the Maginot Line and the Siegfried Line. During the second phase, from December 19 to 25, we were opposed by the 257 Volksgrenadier Division.

Three task forces, composed of infantry-tank teams, were formed under the commands of Lt. Colonel Clayton W. Wells, our 43rd Tank Battalion Commander Major (soon-to-be colonel) Nicholas Novosel, and Major John W. Cunningham. CCA launched the first attack, at 20:00

hours, on December 8 to seize the high ground northeast of Singling. The attack resulted in the capture of two towns and an enemy barracks. Lt. Colonel Clayton Wells' task force captured the town of Singling and moved on to occupy the high ground beyond the town and to consolidate positions. All three of the task forces made separate successful attacks on December 12 that resulted in the capture of the town of Bettviller, the assigned objective. Our 43rd Tank Battalion and the 66th Armored Infantry Battalion took both Guising and Bettviller in daylight attacks.

Our Company B, part of Major Novosel's task force, was sent out on patrol in the vicinity of Singling and moved to a position southwest of Rohrbach where we became bogged down by a wet, cold quagmire of mud. The Germans knew we would be caught in the mud if we left the road, and sure enough, a number of our tanks got stuck in the soft muddy terrain and we were subjected to terrible mortar and artillery fire. Our tank wasn't too far off the edge of the road when we became buried in mud, and the artillery and mortar fire was so severe that we had to stay buttoned up (this was the term used when a tank closed its hatch covers and used periscopes to see). This became intolerable, especially since it was getting dark and we could do nothing but sit there and take it. Darkness, combined with such a limited visual area, made it almost impossible to see anything except for exploding shells and burning tanks. In a lull, when the shelling shifted somewhat, our tank crew decided to risk the shelling and try to get the hell out of there, even though the artillery and mortars were continuing to periodically shell our area.

Our tank crew may have been crazy to take such risks, but the explosions were unceasing and it seemed as though our tank was sinking deeper and deeper in the mud. We decided, risk or no risk, to get out of the mud one way or another. We climbed out of the tank and were able to find some tree trunks and brush, in spite of the darkness, that had been hit and knocked over by enemy shells. We managed to drag them to the tracks, and when we gunned the motors, the tank tracks dragged the brush and tree trunks under the tracks. This gave us enough traction to get us out and back on the road. It was now very dark, and the enemy shelling was much like an annual Fourth of July fireworks display. Because of the circumstances, we were ordered to fall back to Guising, which was out of range of the shelling, and to get some rest and wait for further orders.

9

The order to pull back was a welcome relief. Our only casualties were minor and were due to shrapnel-inflicted wounds while exposed to the shelling. However, we did have a number of cases of trench foot that had been developing along with a few cases of frozen feet, serious enough to result in evacuation from front line duty. (Trench foot is caused by exposure to cold, wetness, and poor circulation and is a painful disorder resembling frostbite. If untreated, it can lead to gangrene.)

Whenever we withdrew out of the attack range of tanks, mortars, artillery, or infantry fire, we soon learned that, unless we were ordered to continue attacking, it was smart to quickly occupy abandoned houses or barns to find places to sleep or for command posts before the rear echelon organizations that follow front-line troops could requisition them.

The weather at this time was getting much worse and had turned miserably wet and cold. The still unfrozen ground was extremely muddy and it had started to snow much harder, so we white-washed our tanks to help conceal them, especially from enemy tanks. Trench foot was becoming a serious problem because our leather combat boots were unsuitable for winter weather. We were equipped as a non-winter vehicular fighting force because greater priority by the U.S. Army commanders had been given to fuel and munitions. Quite simply, the U.S. Army commanders had believed the war in Europe would be over before the onslaught of winter. The lack of shoe-packs or overshoes made conditions extremely difficult to endure. The troops in the infantry usually did not have a problem with body circulation while attacking, but some were unable to leave their foxholes, which were half filled with water and ice, while under attack. Such conditions became so unbearable that many of them became numb, incoherent, and psychologically unfit for combat.

I witnessed this on several occasions when infantry soldiers in their foxholes were like zombies because of the long exposure, incoherent with slurred speech, and had to be led back to the aid station. As tankers, we were able to stay in our tanks, but we also had the same problem of wet, cold feet and were unable to move about to any great extent while in combat action. When conditions were really bad we had to sleep in our tanks, but that was better than sleeping in a snow-filled or water-filled foxhole.

Some units were in the process of getting shoe-packs or over-shoes, but I was not one of the fortunate ones, the main reason probably being that my feet are so damn big. As a result, I got a severe case of trench foot in conjunction with frozen feet in early December before being captured. I took a time-out long enough to build a fire, dry my socks, massage my feet to restore the circulation in my toes, and get the normal color back. While doing this, I refused to carry out one of my sergeant's orders until I had finished. My toes had begun to turn black, and had I not been able to restore the circulation, I could have gotten gangrene and would have had to have my toes amputated. This particular sergeant never did like me, for the likely reason that I had one of the higher IQ's in the division, and although he outranked me, he developed an apparent jealous dislike of me for that reason. The result of all this was that he threatened me with a court-martial.

On December 15, our division, the 12th Armored, in conjunction with the adjacent units, the 87th Infantry Division and the 44th Infantry Division troops, became part of the reserve of Lt. General Alexander Patch's 7th Army and occupied a front that stretched 200 miles from Switzerland to the Saar. The 25th Cavalry Reconnaissance Squadron of the 4th Armored Division relieved the 92nd Cavalry Reconnaissance Squadron. With relief of the division's front lines, the corps boundary was changed and the 80th Infantry Division took over the area formerly occupied by our 12th Armored Division.

We stayed in Guising until December 16 and then returned to Postruff, where some of our troops were billeted in various buildings or were temporarily bivouacked in tents. It was now time to take stock, correct mistakes, and rest up. ("Bivouac" ordinarily means having a tent for cover at night and may have been better than sleeping in the snow on cold, wet ground in the open, but we were not some of the fortunate ones to be billeted in a building or to have a tent at that time.)

Before our crew got a chance to occupy a building for sleeping, we slept in the snow for a couple of nights. This was damn cold, especially during a fresh snowfall. After sleeping in the snow, we were always hungry because of the exposure to the cold and wet, so the few times we were able to get hot food instead of the usual C-Rations and D-bars was a real blessing.

D-bars were chocolate bars filled with God only knows what, vitamins of all kinds encased in chocolate, and they tasted like they looked. They always constipated me terribly, in spite of the fact that most of the time during front line duty troops generally had a problem with the G.I.'s, the term given to the galloping trots or diarrhea. Those few times we were able to get hot, cooked, powdered scrambled eggs were a real blessing.

I once asked our mess sergeant if he ever seasoned the powdered eggs with pepper. He replied "Of course" and proceeded to flick his cigar ashes in the mix. This was a typical Army response, and it didn't seem to make any difference to the taste or to us. Although the powdered eggs were not as good as fresh eggs, they were a damn site better than C-Rations. The scrambled eggs and hot coffee helped to ease the misery. We also had Spam at times, and unlike a lot of Ex-GIs, I liked Spam then and I still do, in spite of the cholesterol. This is probably because of later being worked and nearly starved to death as a prisoner of war.

Considering the alternatives in combat, any warm cooked food was welcome when available. During this short period of rest we had an opportunity not previously available for over four months, and that was to take a hot shower instead of washing and shaving using only cold water placed in our helmets. After four months we had really gotten ripe, and I believe that anyone could have smelled us from ten feet or more away. Luckily, we were trucked to Strasbourg, France, where hot showers had been set up, and this was really a morale booster and delightful. At this time Strasbourg was under American and French control. I didn't know it at the time, but this turned out to be my last shower or bath from the middle of December, 1944, including the Hell Train Ride I was to endure in January, until the middle of April, 1945.

We were also able to read the *Stars & Stripes* (a small newspaper published by the Army that covered the latest events of the war), and of course we were anxious to know if any of our division's exploits had been written up. None had, apparently for security reasons. We later found out that General Eisenhower did not want the Germans to know where the 12th Armored Division was located. To this end, shortly after arriving in France as an armored division, we had been ordered to remove all insignia from our uniforms, tanks, and all personal identifying effects we were carrying in the event of later being captured or to prevent German sympathizers from reporting our location to the Germans. Later on we were also repeatedly reminded to give only our name, rank, and serial number in the event of capture. This meant exactly that, because German intelligence could evaluate even common remarks and relate such remarks to what was going on with the division. I had firsthand knowledge of the importance of such seemingly innocent remarks during my interrogations as a prisoner of war.

Because of the removal of all our insignia and personal identification letters or similar information and the fact that the *Stars & Stripes* was silent as to our actions or location, we later became known as the "Mystery Division" during various press releases because our division was only identified as such. This decision may also have been made for internal political reasons among the Army's higher officer echelon. Regardless of the reasons, I saw a cartoon in *Collier's* magazine after my liberation as a prisoner of war showing a WAC (a member of the Women's Army Corps) with a map pin asking, "On which continent do I place the 12th Armored Division?" The fact that our 44th Tank Battalion of the 12th Armored Division was sent to the Pacific Theatre of operations early in the war may have been a factor, too.

On December 21 we received our first major heavy snowfall and the temperatures at night hovered around zero. We also received some personnel replacements. I always felt sorry for the personnel replacements, because they hadn't been trained with us and didn't understand our operations and as strangers they felt lost and lonesome. Most of the replacements were killed rather quickly because of this. We also exchanged as replacements a number of tanks with 75 mm. guns that had been destroyed or disabled. The newer tanks had the higher velocity 76 mm. gun mountings. As far as I was concerned, this did not make a hell of a lot of difference when compared with the 88 mm. guns that were mounted on the German tanks or those that were drawn by horses or lightly armored vehicles.

At this period of the war, horse drawn guns were becoming more common because the Germans were experiencing fuel shortages. Already we had unwittingly killed a number of horses and cattle that couldn't help getting in the way, and had found that the French were not very ambitious with respect to disposing of their bodies after the battles when the troops had moved on. Instead, they left them rotting where they dropped. Needless to say, the smell was bad and the carcasses were grotesque.

When we began to see the Germans using horses to pull their heavier weapons, we knew they were nearing the end of their fighting days. Nonetheless, we still could do little harm to most of the German tanks with either of our tank-mounted 75 mm. or 76 mm. guns. Without engaging any other enemy forces, we returned to Bettviller, which we had taken on December 12, and we occupied and outposted this town for a number of days without any action.

On Christmas Day, 1944, our mess section prepared an excellent turkey dinner with all the trimmings. Referring to camp kitchens as "the Mess" is not really accurate, at least for most army kitchens during World War II. There were a few exceptions, but the magnificent logistic system that the United States Army was able to sustain so that it could provide, in a combat zone, such a thing as a turkey dinner was unbelievable to the German soldiers. I know it helped my morale a great deal and helped ease the fact that this was my second Christmas away from home. As we celebrated Christmas Day, we coined the motto "Back Alive in '45." Indeed, we were all hopeful we would make it home for the next Christmas.

We had an additional morale booster in one of our fellow tankers, although at times we threatened to kill him. The circumstances were that this fellow tanker had gotten a record player that he could crank up and play. Initially, he had a number of records stored in his tank. After every combat engagement, he would open up the hatch and play a record. The sound of the music had the effect of letting us think about home and that was nice. However, as time went on, all but one record was broken and we were thus blessed with "A Good Man Nowadays Is Hard to Find," sung by Frances Faye.

The problem was that all we heard over and over and over was that same song. It got to the point where we went from laughter upon hearing it to sheer monotony, and soon everyone realized, "Enough is enough!" Whenever we heard that song, we all yelled, "Kill that son-of-a-bitch!" Still, we were in jest, for we knew he had survived and we were reminded of home. A bitching soldier is par for the course, and he never forgets his true purpose as a soldier, in spite of his bitching.

At daylight the morning after Christmas we left Bettviller, France, and started a long cold ride to Lidrizing, France, arriving that evening. We spent the next five days training and running problems with the 66th Infantry Battalion. Just after midnight on New Year's Eve on December 31, 1944, our company commander called us together and with a detailed map of the area pinned to the wall of an abandoned farm house said, "Listen up, men, we have been informed by G2 Army Intelligence that the Germans are going to launch a full scale attack with Tiger tanks, flamethrowers, and infantry. We have been notified to expect that Reichsfuhrer SS Henrich Himmler and his Waffen SS as ordered by Adolph Hitler are planning on launching an attack in Alsace Lorraine to divert Allied pressure from the German forces in their losing battle to retake Bastogne." (Bastogne is a town in southeast Belgium in the Ardennes, and this "losing battle" for the Germans was our great victory the Battle of the Bulge.)

Bloody Herrlisheim was just a few short weeks away.

CHAPTER 2

German Operation Nordwind; 43rd Tank Battalion Attacks Herrlisheim

The series of attacks that began on December 31, 1944, were part of Operation Nordwind. While we had been told that any counteroffensive the Germans could launch would be of little consequence, later on in Herrlisheim we found out differently. As Colonel Nicholas Novosel said to me during his stay in Percy Jones Hospital in Battle Creek, Michigan, after the war, "We were treated as expendables." As such, our battalion was wiped out on January 17, 1945. Colonel Novosel, who reportedly was wounded 17 times during the battle, also said that if he "were given such an order to carry out such a mission ever again," he would refuse and face the consequences rather than have his entire battalion command destroyed as it was at Bloody Herrlisheim, France.

In retrospect, and as reported by *Time Life*,[23] the intelligence officers of the U.S. 7th Army anticipated the attack and warned General Jacob Devers and Dwight Eisenhower of a potential disaster. Ike suggested that Devers withdraw from the threatened area rather than risk the entrapment of his troops. This plan had one major drawback: it meant the French would lose Strasbourg again.

When the French were informed of this plan, they erupted in Gallic furor. Strasbourg had been under German control from 1870 to 1918 and again from 1940 until its liberation in November 1944. The French were fearful of reprisals against the city's 400,000 inhabitants if the Germans returned. Indeed, so alarming was this prospect that the French threatened to remove their forces from Allied control and defend Strasbourg on their own.[24]

"The delicate problem was quickly backed all the way up to Roosevelt and Churchill. Roosevelt refused to become involved, but Churchill discussed the issue in Versailles with Eisenhower, General de Gaulle, and General Alphonse Pierre Juin, chief of staff of the French Ministry of Defense. The Allied leaders decided at the conference to bow to France's wishes and retract the order to abandon Strasbourg. The Allied lines would be shortened, but the city would remain within the area to be defended.[25]

Later on, as a result of this decision, our 43rd Tank Battalion was ordered to attack Herrlisheim and was annihilated. Herrlisheim is about 19 kilometers or 12 miles northeast of Strasbourg. It is also my understanding from subsequent information I received after being released as a prisoner of war that the French failed to attack in unison with our forces and were at least a day late as well. It is sad, considering present-day events, that France has seemingly forgotten the price we Americans paid in freeing her from the Nazis.

On January 8, 1945, we left Lidrizing and drove and slid all night over snow and icy roads for 65 miles, arriving at Kreigsheim early the following morning. Our objective was to stop in Kreigsheim. We were low on gasoline and our supply lines were having difficulty supplying our division and we were ordered to stop our attack. Our artillery, however, was periodically firing a number of 105 mm. and 155 mm. howitzers with the intention of harassing the Germans. This gave us another opportunity to wash and dry our socks over open fires and to warm up again. At this time some of our troops were lucky enough to get shoepacks, overshoes, and winter insulated socks, but a number of our troops were already suffering from trench foot. I was lucky enough to get two pairs of insulated wool socks, and this was a welcome and wonderful relief. I put both pairs on to help keep my feet warm, but I sometimes wondered if I would ever be really warm again.

After arriving in Kreigsheim, which is about 15 km. or nine miles from the Rhine, our company commander was informed that the Germans were attempting to establish a bridgehead west of the Rhine and that we could possibly be encircled by German infantry. Our patrols had also established that the Germans, too, had whitewashed their tanks, and in addition were covering themselves with white sheets so they would blend in with the snow and make it harder for our troops to see them. We were not sure whether or not we had been completely encircled, so we again re-whitewashed our tanks and also formed a circle at night in much the same fashion as the early American pioneers did with their wagon trains as a defensive measure against the Indians.

Company B had been cut off from the rest of the battalion and we had no idea from what direction the Germans might be attacking. In addition, especially since the German attack in the Ardennes, we were aware that the Germans were still sending out English-speaking combat patrol raids in an operation known as "Operation Greif" that I believe in German means "Victory is within reach," with soldiers dressed in American uniforms as infantry troops and as American M.P.'s (military police) who changed road signs and gave false directions to American vehicular traffic to disrupt and confuse our troops. It was thus very important that we challenge anyone and everyone approaching in the darkness or during the daylight, and if they did not know the password, they were immediately taken into custody and transported back to our command post.

Although things were seemingly quiet, I was selected to nightly move out of our defensive circle on outpost duty taking a bag of 45 caliber clips for my grease gun (a machine gun shaped like a grease gun) and a bag of hand grenades. My job was to warn of any German patrols or enemy movement that might occur and to fire at any enemy patrol and to throw grenades to give a wake-up call to the company. This was part of a nightly routine procedure of guard duty to keep sleeping tankers from getting their throats cut by German patrols. Incidentally, this did happen to some sleeping crews who had not properly posted guards or when the guards had fallen asleep.

However, I was being selected too many consecutive nights until I reached the conclusion that my sergeant was trying to save his own ass or was hoping to get me killed rather than spread the duty around. We did not always see eye to eye, and I finally decided enough of this shit. I threatened him by placing my M3-A1 45-caliber grease gun in his face and saying, "Unless you start giving other soldiers the same wonderful opportunity to become a hero, or at least send out two of us at a time so we would have a better chance of survival in the event that we are caught or challenged by a German patrol, I'll blow your God-damned head off." Needless to say he avoided further contact with me and filed an official charge against me for a general court-martial. However, my captain knew that the circumstances as I expressed them were correct, and he refused to proceed with the charges during the heat of combat.

Those of us who survived the forthcoming battle at Herrlisheim were taken prisoner, and that solved the pending general court-martial problem. Later, as a prisoner of war, in a temporary holding area and as an enlisted soldier, prior to being separated from the officers, my captain and a full colonel of the 79th division who was also a prisoner of war asked me to help plan an escape with them. That to me verified my captain's faith in me as a soldier. Unfortunately, we did not get the opportunity to attempt our escape before we were separated and sent to different, more secure, permanent prison camps. It was a policy of the Germans under the terms of the Geneva Convention to separate enlisted men from the officers as prisoners of war during their imprisonment.

I had been placed at a roadblock with two others of our tank crew on January 9, 1945, during this period in which we were not certain whether or not the Germans would try to infiltrate our area, when we stopped a jeep. I trained my bazooka on the jeep and when the officer did not know the latest password, we had him escorted back to our command post. He actually was a full colonel and did not know the present battalion password. At the command post he properly identified himself, and instead of criticizing us or chewing us out, he told the officers at the command post to pass along his compliments to us for doing our job. (By the way, it took two of us to load and fire our bazookas, whereas the German *panzerfaust* could be loaded and fired by one individual. It was the *panzerfaust* that was used extensively in the Battle of Berlin by the German Volkstrum [Peoples' Army.])

Fortunately, our battalion was correct in at least one instance, when we stopped a German dressed in an American uniform who spoke excellent English with an American accent and did know the correct password. Because he acted very suspiciously, he was taken prisoner and was sent back to the command post for further questioning. Later, we found out that he was indeed a German. How he obtained our current password was a mystery, but it may have been from a German patrol close enough at night to overhear the password and counter sign, although the passwords were continually being changed. We also found out through our intelligence that the Germans were being helped by a few sympathetic citizens among the Alsatian population. That was the reason we changed our passwords on a regular basis, sometimes twice a day. Those identified as Germans in American uniforms were classified as spies and shot almost immediately.

Another very interesting event involved an American jeep carrying five Germans dressed as American soldiers who were riding in our column during our company movement. The jeep was traveling in and out of our column and no one seemed to know who the hell was in it. Eventually it was stopped, and we found out the soldiers were part of the German "Operation Greif" Program. Identified as spies, they were executed by firing squad.

The month of January, 1945, was the bloodiest chapter of the 12th Armored Division. This memorable period lasted from January 8 to 20. During this action we reached one of our assigned objectives, the town of Herrlisheim, but each time we attacked we were forced to withdraw because we were outnumbered in men and equipment.

(The town of Herrlisheim is located about 25 km. (16 miles) northeast of Strasbourg. For some reason, Herrlisheim does not appear on many French maps. I found this out when I re-visited France in 1994, when a number of people in Strasbourg did not seem to know of the village of Herrlisheim. Nonetheless, I was pleased to know that the people of Herrlisheim have maintained a museum of data and facts commemorating our battalion's annihilation. The community has great respect for America for liberating them from the Nazis in World War II. I had an enjoyable meeting with their mayor, Louis Becker, who spoke very good English. Although he was too young to remember World War II, he showed us a plaque in the courthouse together with a stone monument of the church that was destroyed in the town square.)

We had been led to believe that Herrlisheim was held by second-rate young kids and older soldiers with little firepower, according to Army intelligence. (Somehow, our intelligence system doesn't seem to improve with time or location.) On the contrary, as mentioned earlier, the bloody battle at Herrlisheim was tied up with Von Rundstedt's Wacht am Rhein offensive in the Ardennes.

When this operation failed, von Rundstedt withdrew eight divisions from the northern sector of the Ardennes and transported them to the northern border of Alsace Lorraine to the small bridgehead the Germans had established in the small sector between Strasbourg and the Maginot Line, centering in the villages of Gambsheim and Herrlisheim. (This was Operation Nordwind, later to be known as "The Little Bulge.")

The German objective was to recapture Strasbourg and move through the Saverne Gap behind the Allied lines. The Germans had concluded that the American withdrawal from the bridgeheads in the Saar River area and the forces opposing them on this front south from the Ardennes had been seriously weakened by the Ardennes offensive. The German Army Group G had therefore been directed to exploit the situation, mounting local attacks in readiness for a general offensive.

Early on the foggy morning of January 16, our division renewed its attack on Herrlisheim, and our Company B of the 43rd Tank Battalion along with the 17th Armored Infantry Battalion attacked enemy positions in the Steinwald woods and near the open plain north of the woods. As we pulled up for position prior to our attack, we could see two burning tanks on the open plain, about two thousand feet away, that had been knocked out earlier and that may have been from the 714th Tank Battalion that earlier had been subjected to intense enemy tank and artillery fire.

Even though we were in an active battle zone and were being subjected to enemy infantry and intermittent artillery, tank, and mortar fire, I was ordered to leave my tank and investigate the burning tanks to see if there were any wounded survivors still in them. This I did, utilizing my earlier training in infantry tactics by running in bursts and hitting the ground and rolling over in the snow, and I mean hugging the ground after rolling in order to avoid enemy rifle fire. The snow did not help, because I was dressed in an olive drab uniform and this showed up easily in the white snow. Our tank commander did not want to risk exposing our tanks any more than was absolutely necessary, so as usual I was sent out alone. That goes along with the old saying, "Shit flows downhill." As luck would have it, I succeeded in reaching the tanks without being hit by small arms fire, although the German troops were trying like hell.

Both tanks had been hit and had exploded and were still burning slowly. Each tank held a dead tanker, and there were some dead German infantry lying nearby, but there were no living or wounded survivors in either tank and there wasn't anything I could do under the circumstances, since we were getting ready to renew our attack. Now all I had to do was to try to get back to my tank alive. I successfully returned to my tank in the same manner, except that now I was not only cold but wet from the snow as well.

Fortunately, although I was subjected to burp gun and machine gun fire, it wasn't real intense and they weren't able to get me directly in their sights. At least they didn't waste a 88 mm. shell with delayed action fuses on me like they had been doing to effectively work over our infantry. I use the word "waste" because firing a 88 mm. shell at a single soldier was considered wasteful and expensive. It was more efficient to kill a single soldier with small arms fire rather than to use such a large, expensive shell. The Germans had a limited supply of shells and had to use them extremely carefully, although I did at times see such a thing and we were guilty as well at times of picking off an individual German with a tank shell. Once during the fall we tracked and successfully fired our tank gun at a German soldier on a motorcycle at a distance of approximately a mile, blowing him sky high.

There had been sporadic bursts of small arms, machine gun fire, and mortar fire earlier, and our company tanks were spread out along the edge of the open plain and were returning fire from both our 75 mm. gun and the 50-caliber machine gun mounted on the top of our tank while waiting to launch another major tank attack.

Our tank had been firing at enemy positions when a German Mark IV tank pulled out from the edge of the woods and was broadside to our line of fire. We fired an armor piercing shell and hit the side just above the track and succeeded in penetrating the armor at a weak point, disabling the tank and starting it to burn. Shortly thereafter things quieted down, and as a bow gunner at that time with the temperature close to zero, I was plagued with the fact that I had the G.I.'s. In plain English, I couldn't hold it any longer and I had to shit or suffer sitting in it while waiting to launch another attack.

During a lull in the intermittent firing, I asked the driver to hold fast and I got out of the tank and relieved myself as close to the tank tracks as I could. I could hear the response of our company commander, who was somewhere in a tank towards our rear. Although he was yelling over the tank radio, I could also hear him without benefit of the radio. He was loudly screaming and swearing while asking, "Who the hell is that dumb son-of-a-bitch?" and "Get that dumb bastard back in the tank," etc.

This was probably very stupid on my part, but as a typical twenty-year-old, I felt I was invulnerable and that I would live forever. When I finished, I got back in the tank. This may come as a surprise to a lot of people, but during that interval the enemy soldiers did not fire at me, and they definitely could have with small arms fire. I believe they deliberately considered a time out, probably thinking that any dumb son-of-a-bitch who would expose himself under such conditions should be left alone to do his business.

I experienced other instances such as this with some of the front line troops of the Wehrmacht. Some of them were decent soldiers, and there were even a few SS troops who abided by the Geneva Convention rules. I use the word "few," wherein chivalry was not totally dead. I learned later as a prisoner of war that the German combat soldiers in general had honor, discipline, and respect for their enemies. Likewise, the German Wehrmacht soldiers did, by and large, follow the terms and conditions of the Geneva Convention a hell of a lot better than those Waffen

SS bastards who were in charge of most of the prisoner of war camps, the forced labor camps, and the death camps in Germany itself. These same SS troops were also the troops responsible for the Holocaust.

Because we were still under active combat conditions, we spent the night of January 16 in our tanks and we did not leave our engines running for warmth. The weather was terribly cold and we still did not have shoepacks. In addition, my feet were still bothering me from the effects of trench foot and frostbite in early December. I had managed previously to get my overcoat and, like the infantry, I put it on over my field jacket in spite of having to squeeze into my seat in the tank. On the cold foggy morning of January 17, while standing outside our lead tank and waiting for orders to renew the attack on Herrlisheim, an officer in a jeep approached from the rear in haste. He came up to me and saluted and asked, "Sir, when is your force going to attack?" I returned his salute and said, "The plan is to attack at about 08:00 hours." He said "Thank you, sir," saluted, and left.

This shows some of the confusion that can occur. Apparently, since I was the only one wearing an overcoat, he assumed I was the commanding officer. With all due respect, he had to be inexperienced, because if I were the commanding officer, I sure as hell would not have been in the lead tank. Why he wanted to know was a mystery, and I never found out what outfit he was in. (Officers did not openly show or visibly display their rank in the combat zones because of enemy snipers.)

At or about 08:00 on January 17, we were again ordered to re-attack, and this operation proved to be sheer madness and the most costly one we encountered in the history of the division. As a result of this attack, the Germans called the 12th Armored the "Suicide Division." The other two platoons of our company had the mission of guarding the left flank of the 43rd Tank Battalion, whose objective was the town of Offendorf, only about two km. (1.2 miles) southeast of Herrilisheim. One platoon was supporting both the A and B Companies of the 66th Infantry Battalion. The 66th Infantry Battalion's objective was to secure the Steinwald Woods, thus securing the right flank of the 43rd Tank Battalion.

Contrary to earlier reports of our G2 divisional intelligence stating that we could expect little or no resistance in Herrlisheim because the present-day German soldiers were mostly old men and boys, there was plenty of resistance. This bullshit must have been given to us to encourage us to attack without due caution. We learned the hard way that the Germans we were attacking outnumbered us in troops, tanks, and equipment and were well trained, hardened, experienced soldiers. They sure as hell were not second-rate soldiers or kids but were part of the 10th SS Division made up of hardened battle veterans. Our battalion had already lost 12 tanks the previous day in trying to take Herrlisheim from these so-called second-rate troops.

My tank began the attack by approaching Herrlisheim north of the Steinwald woods and in a northwesterly direction. All hell seemed to break loose while we were crossing the railroad heading for the main part of town. Just as we were going up over the railroad grade, we were fired on by the 88 mm. gun of a Tiger tank somewhere off to our right rear flank. It came as a total surprise, since we had no idea where in hell the Germans were located. The first shot was so close to my turret hatch, which was still open, that I could actually feel the heat from the shell on the back of my neck. If I had been fully sitting up in the hatch it would have taken my head off, as I had witnessed happening to a tank commander on another occasion.

I was seated in the turret and my job was assistant gunner and loader. At that time we had the later version of the Sherman tank that had an additional hatch on the left side of the tank turret directly above the loader's seat. Since the shell did not hit our tank, we were able to go down the embankment without further enemy fire until we were further into the downtown area.

As our tank moved slowly toward the downtown area in column formation, we were subjected to enemy infantry fire, including the German bazooka known as the *panzerfaust*. Quite simply, we were ambushed as we approached the downtown area. A number of infantry from the 17th Armored Infantry Battalion were following our tank, some were walking behind our tank, and some were even riding on top, still under the belief that we were facing second-rate troops. I believe some of the infantry were from the B 119th engineer company and were being used as infantry in alleviating the 56 AIB (Armored Infantry Battalion).

Before we had gotten very far and were buttoned up, we could see these poor bastards being killed right on top of and in the back of our tank. We couldn't do a damn thing about it, because we could not see exactly where the small arms fire or the 88 mm. gunfire was coming from to enable us to return either machine gun or tank gun fire.

How did we know we were being fired on by 88 mm. guns? We recognized the sound of the shells and also witnessed their results when they struck either a tank or building. It was a bloody mess, with the infantry being riddled by machine guns that couldn't as yet be seen. It was like Dante's Inferno with all the explosions, burning bombed-out buildings, and the killing of the exposed infantry and engineers. Fortunately, as we moved down the road, I saw a window shade on the second floor of a building at the end of the street being pulled down and then raised, apparently as some sort of a signal, because as soon as it happened we were fired on again from our right rear flank.

CHAPTER 3

43rd Tank Battalion Survivors Surrender

Our tank was the lead tank in a column approaching and attacking Herrlisheim in the central business district, and with the signal that appeared to have been given, the 88 mm. gun somewhere to our right rear fired at the rear of our column like a turkey shoot, getting the tanks in back of us first, much to the chagrin of the officers who generally avoided the lead tanks and were now receiving concentrated fire more than we were. Since I believed that the curtain shade was a signal from a German forward observer, I told the 76 mm. gunner to sight on the window while I loaded a HE (high explosive) shell and to fire at the window in the second story. He did, and the blast and explosion from our 76 mm. gun silenced their forward observer and obliterated the whole second story, setting the building on fire.

The enemy fire was still excessive and terribly costly to our tanks and supporting infantry and engineers. It's not a pleasant sight to see your supporting infantrymen being killed and wounded in front of your very eyes, and at the same time not being able to do anything but try to see the enemy while looking through a periscope. During this period of time, our supporting infantry were busy trying to survive and were unable to act as our eyes.

This was an experience a soldier always remembers. Your eyes bug out straining to see your enemy first, your throat is dry, the palms of your hands actually sweat, and your heart beats like a trip hammer, because you must see him before he sees you and fire, if you can, your inferior tank shells before he fires a deadly shell at you. At the same time, if you are unable to see him and he fires first, you become the victim.

Our troops had given our tanks the nickname the "Ronsons" after the cigarette lighter by the same name because when we were hit directly, the German 88 mm. shells penetrated our tanks unless we were lucky enough to receive a glancing hit. When the German 88 mm. armor-piercing shell did strike our tanks directly, the shell generally went on through our armament. It usually exploded and started the tank on fire, which is why the name "Ronson" became a popular expression among our troops. As a tank crew member, if you were lucky enough to survive the hit and explosion, the next problem was to escape through the hatches without being shot by enemy infantry or snipers. Our tanks did have an escape plate on the bottom of the tank that we could open and let drop and then crawl out through, much like getting through a manhole. The only problem was that most of the time the tanks were either in soft ground or on a muddy road so that if you did open the escape hatch, the tank tracks were submerged enough in the ground or mud so that escape was impossible for lack of clearance.

We were ordered to continue to move to the downtown area, in spite of the 88 mm. fire coming from our rear right flank. As we did so, we came to a major street intersection with two-story buildings at all four corners. That made it impossible for us to see what was lying either to the right or to the left of the street intersection. We could only guess that more than likely they were waiting to the right or left of the intersection for us to pull up into the intersection and fire directly at us from a Tiger tank or an 88 mm. anti-tank gun or a *panzerfaust* as soon as we became visible. There were enough two-story buildings blocking the view from our direction so that we had no way of knowing what to expect, and most of the infantry that had been accompanying us and acting as our eyes while we were buttoned up had already been shot and wounded or killed. Our tank commander suspected that if we pulled up to the intersection, they would fire at us directly with an anti-tank gun. More than likely they had already zeroed in on whatever came past the corner so that they couldn't miss.

Our tank commander wisely told our driver, when ready, to gun the shit out of the tank engines and head for the other side of the intersection within the protection of the buildings on the opposite side of the street intersection in as few seconds as possible so we would have a chance of not being hit. Our driver did exactly that and, sure enough, we had crossed the open area of the intersection in a matter of seconds. They fired almost instantly but they missed us, though not by much. Successfully clearing the intersection did not accomplish much, because we did not have enough able infantry support to knock out any German gun emplacement by killing their operators and our tank could not get into a firing position without first being fired on by the 88 mm. gun hidden from our view away from the street intersection on our left flank, located on the street we had just crossed.

Our orders were to move forward and attack regardless, bypassing any such gun installation, so we followed orders. Unfortunately, we could not proceed further up the street because we did not have enough infantry support to protect our rear. All in all, it was one hell of a situation in which to hope to survive, and the other tanks in our column would have the same problem with the same intersection where that particular 88 mm. anti-tank gun was located. Our problem now was to try to get back across the intersection and to locate the 88 mm. gun that was destroying the tanks to our right rear flank.

Our tank commander made the decision to move back through the intersection in the same way we had crossed in the first place and to try to locate the gun emplacement at our right rear flank and make every effort to silence the bastard if possible one way or another. We gunned the shit out of our tank engines and successfully backed through the

31

intersection, much to the surprise of the Germans. They apparently did not expect us to move back. We were unable to locate the 88 mm. gun in spite of firing at locations that appeared to have flash points. (Flash points were points that indicated the firing of a larger gun by the visible presence of a flash of light prior to hearing an explosion. Most of the German tanks, like ours, had flash hiders on the ends of their barrels that generally concealed any such flashes, so what we saw was probably from another type of heavy gun.)

We found out too late as we were being rounded up as prisoners of war that the gun that had been firing at our rear was a German Tiger tank that had been dug into the ground or was in the basement of a building that had been destroyed so that the only part of it that was exposed was the turret and gun. The tracks were not visible, and if we had seen it in time, we still could not have knocked it out with our 76 mm. gun.

The upper part of the German tank turret was not vulnerable because of its thick steel armament, and what was left of our infantry was unable to locate or silence the gun by bazookas or flamethrowers. As a result, we became separated from the rest of the tank column. We also could not get the German gun that was located on the westerly side of the intersection, because even if we did rush the street where it was, they could fire instantly before we could even attempt to aim and fire.

It probably would not have made much difference anyway, because we were being subjected to murderous fire from the same general direction to our right rear flank where the Tiger tank was dug in. At the time we could not see or figure out where in hell it was hidden. We had thought it might be in the basement of one of the buildings with just enough exposure to be able to fire without giving itself away, and that the 17th Armored Infantry Battalion was in back of us and still returning fire at enemy positions that were firing at us with small arms, mortars, and some artillery.

Unfortunately, the 17th Armored Infantry Battalion was having as much trouble as we were in trying to locate and isolate the German fire-power coming from their tanks and anti-tank guns. Two of our tanks were now separated somewhat from the rest of the column and we were not sure exactly which ones could still fight.

Our tank remained in this position for some time, firing at whatever we thought was either an enemy gun location or small arms fire by observing the flash points. We were engaged in street fighting, firing the 76 mm. gun directly at enemy troops along with the 50-caliber machine gun and the 30-caliber machine gun in the front bow of the tank. We fired at anything that moved in the bombed-out buildings and rubble piles that we knew were occupied by Germans. However, we were under strength, thanks to the previous day's action in which 12 tanks had been knocked out and 11 others badly damaged. In addition, we were greatly outnumbered by the Germans, who were in an ambush position and extremely well camouflaged. Later on in the afternoon, a vacant building near the area where the last of our five tanks were destroyed was to become our command post.

Our tank was in this position for some time and we continued to sweep the area with continuous fire until a German Tiger tank started to approach us directly, coming down the street where we were initially headed. We rapidly fired at least five successive rounds from our 76 mm. gun directly at the Tiger tank. The shells glanced off harmlessly as they slowly traversed their 88 mm. gun, got us in their sights, and fired. There wasn't a damn thing we could do about it, and we could not get the hell out of their way because we were blocked by buildings that we could not push through or over. Needless to say, they did not miss us this time. The shots we fired did no harm whatsoever and did not scare them off as we had been able to do in past tank battles with lighter German tanks or with the regular Wehrmacht armored division.

The next thing I knew, an 88 mm. armor-piercing shell hit the front of our tank at the bow gunner's location, in the lower right hand side of the tank. The shell went right on through the tank and the bow gunner. As fate would have it, I had been in that position the day before when our battalion had lost 12 tanks. We often had to change positions as crew members because of personnel losses. Our bow gunner didn't know what hit him, and there wasn't much left of him because of the size of the shell. The noise of the explosion was deafening inside the tank. In those days, we did not have any ear protection, even when firing our 75 mm. or 76 mm. guns. It's a wonder we didn't lose our hearing, although on some days after firing either the 75 mm. or 76 mm. gun while buttoned up, we were unable to hear each other, without yelling, for several hours afterwards.

The incoming shell exploded after impact and started our tank on fire. Before the tank exploded from gasoline followed by exploding shells stored under the floor of the tank turret, we were ordered by our tank commander to abandon the tank and try to get back towards where the center of the column had originally been located, even though by this time most of the tanks to our rear had been destroyed, disabled, or were on fire by what I referred to earlier as a turkey shoot.

Two tanks were still left near the original center of the town, still firing at enemy infantry and still trying to locate the 88 mm. gun or guns that were off to our rear right flank. When our tank commander told us to abandon our tank, I grabbed two smoke grenades and tossed them out of the tank on two sides to give us as much smoke cover as possible. I then grabbed my grease gun and stuffed a couple of 45 caliber clips in my jacket that was underneath my coat and actually dove out of the upper turret hatch in the area of thick smoke, landing outside near the side rear, damn near spraining my wrists. They weren't sprained, but they hurt like hell. That surprised me, because typically in such circumstances you don't notice much pain until later. I wasn't hit with enemy fire at this time, but afterward I noticed that the front of my coat was full of bullet holes close enough to my stomach to burn my skin. I was unbelievably lucky. Our tank commander and two of us survived and were later taken prisoner.

After I dove out of the tank I fired at every son-of-a-bitch I could see who was trying to shoot me first, much like the old wild west shoot out. I have no idea how many soldiers I hit or killed or wounded. I was able to see periodically and only briefly enemy infantry soldiers who had white bed sheets covering most of their regular army uniforms so that they would blend in with the snow and who were firing at me from bombed out buildings along the street. In these areas the white bed sheets did not conceal them too much, but when they were in the snowdrifts or in areas of snow cover in the streets, it was damn difficult to see them and get them in your gun sights.

Believe me, it is some experience, knowing that at any time you could be killed. I continued to return fire until I had used up about half of my 45 caliber clips, and then I crawled (hugged the ground) towards a tank that was still firing a 50-caliber machine gun. When I no longer had any ammunition, I began to crawl towards the tank to my rear along the edge of a brick fence wall that was about three feet high. I could see a German soldier aiming at me, trying like hell to get me in his sights without over-exposing himself to the 50-caliber gunner who was giving me fire cover. This is not the most pleasant situation in the world to be in, but I believed what my platoon sergeant during training had always told me, and in my mind I could hear him saying "Hug the ground, hug the ground" or crawl under something when in such a situation.

During basic training, our sergeant used to jump on our heads and necks with both of his feet when we were training in the desert to emphasize the fact that we had to keep our heads down to survive. The German could not quite get his rifle up high enough to aim above the brick wall without exposing himself too much to the surviving tank commander, who was laying down a covering fire with his 50-caliber machine gun. This same sergeant saved my life because of his intense fire directed at those sons-of-bitches who were bent on killing us. Sadly, this same sergeant continued to fire until he was killed by enemy fire. All during this time he was exposed but continued to fire until he was killed. Such bravery should have been recognized and so honored, but the circumstances that followed prevented such recognition, particularly since our 43rd Battalion was wiped out during this battle.

The German did not succeed in hitting me fatally, but he was able to shoot me in the arm. Luckily, the other bullets only burned the surface of my skin, and I managed to keep on crawling because I realized what the alternative would be. Our tank driver who was right behind me did not make it. Riddled with bullets, he apparently had not kept low enough while crawling or close enough to the brick fence. Since I had been shot and was bleeding quite badly, this same tank commander yelled to me before he was killed, pointing to where the command post was now located in a building nearby, that I could have my wounds bandaged there.

At about 12:30 p.m. on Wednesday, January 17, 1945, our company commander's tank had been hit by enemy fire and was completely disabled and set on fire but he managed to get out of the tank alive and set up a command post in a nearby building as a defense to try to hold out against the attacking German forces. The building was a fairly large French-type farmhouse that was within the village limits of Herrlisheim. Now limited to walkie-talkie radio communications, he began trying to conduct some semblance of infantry operations from this building with the surviving tankers using sub-machine guns in conjunction with a couple of surviving armored infantry that had also made it to the building. The hope was that the earlier request made to division headquarters by Colonel Novosel for additional support infantry and tanks would be fulfilled before we were completely wiped out by superior German forces.

I succeeded in making it into the command post and was directed by our company commander to go to the cellar where a medic was treating other wounded soldiers, including a couple of captured German enlisted men. I did as I was directed and went down a rickety stairway to the cellar. The cellar had a dirt floor and the only light was from lanterns and candles that had been in the farmhouse. There was no electric service; everything had been knocked out in the village. In the cellar were several soldiers who had died from wounds, both German and American. The medic treated my wounds with sulfa and bandaged me and managed to stop the bleeding. I did not take a morphine serrate since my pain was minimal because of shock, but my arm was numb and I couldn't move it.

Though dingy and poorly lighted, the cellar was a temporary haven for the wounded. The two German soldiers who had been wounded were being held by us there. Two of our tankers and two soldiers from the 17th Armored Infantry were also there, suffering and bleeding badly. There wasn't much the medic or anyone else could do for them. The tanker, whom I knew from our company, was dying, and I offered him a cigarette that he struggled to accept. I lit it for him, and as I did so one of the Germans said to me "Haben sie zigaretten?" In a situation such as this deep-seated feelings of animosity are no longer present, at least among the suffering, and I did give each of them a cigarette to which they replied "Danke schon." No more was said.

The medic had just completed bandaging me when our captain hollered down to the cellar, "Muscles, you speak some German, so get your ass up here as soon as you can; we have captured a German officer and we need some information from him." I complied without hesitation because I personally had a great deal of respect and admiration for our captain. The nickname "Muscles" was not just an outgrowth of my last name, but became my nickname in our company when I demonstrated that I could lift and carry a tank bogey wheel that weighed several hundred pounds.

When I got up to the captain he was standing with the German officer and he said to me, "We need to know more about what in hell we are up against both in numbers and which divisions are facing us."

As our captain requested, I asked the German officer how many tanks, supporting infantry, and which German divisions were up against us. The officer was afraid, and the only answer we could get from him was his rank and serial number, along with his requested assurance that we would treat him as an officer and a gentlemen and that we would adhere to the Articles of the Geneva Convention pertaining to prisoners of war. Although our captain did a lot of swearing and referred to him as a son-of-a-bitch and a Nazi bastard, we were unable to get any useful information from him. It was obvious that he didn't speak or understand English, because of the names our captain was calling him. We did, however, treat him with respect and this probably saved our lives as I will explain later on.

By this time the few remaining 28 operational tanks that we had started out with that morning were encountering deadly anti-tank fire and our losses mounted steadily. Before the day was over, a grand total of 62 of our battalion tanks had been destroyed or disabled in two days. Some of the tanks on the edge of town had broken through the ice and frozen ground and were mired down in the mud, easy targets. This was another indication as to the importance of established roadways. The infantry encountered heavy artillery fire and small arms fire from protected positions of ambush that riddled their ranks and prevented them from reaching their objectives. In addition, toward the end of the day, the infantry was subjected to an enemy shelling of white phosphorous.

If you had high school chemistry, you know what a terrible burn it makes when it comes in contact with your skin. Unless immediate medical treatment is given, the phosphorous continues to burn and penetrate to your bloodstream with terrible pain before causing death. One of the infantryman, later a prisoner of war in a German prison camp, told me about losing some of his men in this way, describing it as a terrible agony for the dying soldiers.

Despite our losses in men and tanks, the battalion was ordered to continue fighting towards their objective until overcome. I don't remember the exact time when we heard the last radio message from Colonel Novosel, who was somewhere within a block or so of us, when he said "Things are getting hot," but it was sometime in the afternoon. It was the evening of the 17th, and we were taken prisoner just as it was getting dark in the town of Herrilisheim.

Our surrender of the command post was ordered by our captain after a Tiger tank pulled up directly in front of the building we were in and gave us an opportunity to surrender before firing their tank gun. I believe they knew we had a German officer prisoner and that we also held some other German soldiers. The German officer we held informed us that he would help us surrender without any further bloodshed, since any continued resistance would be futile since there was no way in hell we could cope with a Tiger tank. At this point we had nothing left to fight with, no small arms ammunition and no bazooka or anything else to fire or throw at their tank. Our captain agreed to surrender and the German officer turned us over to the German troops outside our temporary command post.

We were ordered to assemble in front of the building with our hands up in the air, and they instructed us to bring up our wounded along with the German wounded that we had in the cellar. Because of my wounds in my right arm, the Germans permitted me to leave my arm dangling down even though I did not have a sling. Hell, I couldn't raise it up anyway. I continued as a walking wounded, and I was instructed to go over to where Colonel Novosel was lying with the other wounded and helped arrange to carry him using my one good arm. We carried him to a barge on the river Rhine where we were transported across. We had found an old wooden ladder in the village and used that as a stretcher to carry him. As a walking wounded, I helped carry the ladder that he was on using my left hand and arm that was still all right. By this time it was dark and the flames of the burning and smoking buildings and the dead and bloody soldiers amid the flickering shadows was like being at the gates of hell. It was a very depressing time to have to surrender to the enemy. The German soldiers were hardy and healthy looking young men with excellent physical stature and were grinning at us because they had forced us to surrender.

After being lined up, we were ordered to march to the barge on the Rhine, about two miles away. As we began to do so, we approached a large truck directly in the center of the road that had a canvas cover hanging from the back of the truck. As we got closer, the guards accompanying us stepped further to the sides of the road. We already knew about the Malmedy, Belgium, massacre that had occurred similarly, and I thought, "Well, this is going to be it for us." It had all the markings of a set-up that would enable German soldiers to open the canvas cover on the truck and mow us down with a machine gun rather than take us prisoner. I was preparing for the worst when the officer we had held as a captive came running up yelling, "*Nein, nein, ich habe mein wort als offizier und ehrenmann gegeben, diese Gefangenen der Deutschen kommandantur als kriegsgefangene zu ubergeben.*" ("No, no, I gave my word as an officer and a gentlemen to turn these prisoners over to the German command as prisoners of war.") He kept his word to us because we had honored the terms of the Geneva Convention when the situation was reversed. No more was said, and the German guards closed ranks and we continued to walk, bypassing the truck with the canvas back drop, and carrying our colonel on the improvised ladder as a stretcher.

The small group of men I marched with were all able-bodied and had surrendered at the command post. The barge we marched to was a small one with a pair of outboard motors. After we were loaded on the barge, we made the trip across. It was getting colder as darkness descended and of course we had had nothing to eat since early morning the day before. Conditions were very depressing to say the least. We crossed the Rhine and walked a little over two miles more to a building that I believe was being used as a German barracks. The Germans took the colonel and some other more severely wounded men who were unable to walk to a German medical field hospital, and I never saw the colonel again until I visited him at the Percy Jones Hospital in Battle Creek, Michigan, during the fall of 1945. I took my chances by refusing to go with the other wounded. At the time I wanted to stay with our small group, and I felt, why trust some other bastards?

When we got to the German barracks they took us into an adjoining horse barn nearby where we were told to bed down in the stable area near the horses. It was a relief to get inside and out of the snow and cold sharp wind. Hunger and the wish for a cigarette was really nagging at us. The Germans had no intention of giving us any food or water prior to being interrogated, though while walking to the barracks we had been able to periodically grab handfuls of snow to quench our thirst.

CHAPTER 4

Imprisoned at
Stalag X1 B

We spent the night in the horse barn sleeping on the ground in some hay, and early the next morning we were taken to an office in the barracks and were individually interrogated by a dapper looking German officer of the 10th SS Panzer Division who spoke excellent English. We still had not received any food or water, and by this time I was dying for a cigarette. The German officer was sitting at a desk enjoying a cigarette, and on the desk were cigarettes and a bowl of apples along with the remains of the breakfast he had been enjoying. By this time anything looked good. He began questioning me while blowing fragrant smelling tobacco smoke towards me in an antagonizing manner. As instructed by our officers, I gave only my name, rank, and serial number. It became apparent that what the Germans were interested in primarily was where we were getting our gasoline for our tanks and motorized vehicles. We knew that they were operating with extremely limited gasoline supplies, whereas our army seemed to have an unlimited supply. The Germans' plan was to capture as much gasoline as possible while attacking during their offensive action.

Soon the questioning became more severe, with the added threat of violence. Since I did not give any additional information, the officer had a rough looking corporal repeatedly hit me in the head and face with his rifle butt along with his fists. I lost one of my upper front teeth later on as a result of this. I remained conscious but refused to make any other comments. He said, "You know that I can have you shot." I told him I did not know where our gasoline was coming from, and I reminded him that we had observed the Geneva Convention with the captured German officer we had held prior to our surrender.

After a series of threats and physical slugfests, he appeared to soften and tried the good treatment policy, offering me a cigarette and saying that if I were cooperative, he would see that I got some food and better treatment later on. As much as I wanted to, I did not accept the cigarette. None of us liked the black German cigarettes anyway. Since I did not give any additional information, he finally gave up on me and sent me back with the rest of our group and continued to interrogate the rest of the prisoners.

I don't know what the results were, but I learned later that innocent comments when collected and analyzed often led to sources of information, such as a comment I heard from one of our group, who answered the question as to where we got our gasoline by stating "Out of five-gallon cans." This apparent wise-ass answer was helpful to the Germans, because that is where we did get our gasoline, and it told them we probably were being supplied by trucks. That in turn narrowed down the distance and potential location of gas dumps that could be reached by suitable roads, and not just to what we often referred to as two-track dirt roads that were common in the area of Alsace Lorraine.

The interrogations were over in about an hour and we were then lined up in a column of twos. We had been walking easterly through the farmland for about six km. (3.6 miles) when we passed the outskirts of the village of Rhein-Munster. Our only source of water was still handfuls of snow we grabbed as we walked along in the cold. The Germans had taken my overcoat, leaving me with only my field jacket, but I was able to keep my wool cap. This meant a great deal later because it helped keep my head warm and my ears from freezing. They took just about everything else, too, but I had kept my razor packet in my side pocket and this I also was able to keep, and I used this later to keep shaven. I learned how to sharpen my blade on my belt in the prison camp and this worked somewhat. At least I attempted to look like a soldier, a term often used by General Patton. I also had leather field boots that were not for winter wear, and the previous results of my trench foot were getting worse. Although the scenery was beautiful and it would have been an enjoyable walk under different circumstances, the penetrating cold with subzero temperatures was miserable and I wondered as I did many times later on whether I would ever get warm again this side of hell.

We continued walking easterly and in the afternoon we came to the outskirts of Baden-Baden in the northwest corner of the Black Forest. "*Baden*" means "have a bath." We had seen the signs and already knew that this was a resort town famous for its mineral baths. We did not stop but continued walking easterly, and we still hadn't received any food or water other than the snow we grabbed as we walked along. Sometime after dark on January 18, 1945, we reached the village of Bad Wildbad, about 40 km. (25 miles) from where we had been interrogated early that morning. I learned that the Army's reason for having us train for such hikes had plenty of merit. I know that we were all cold, hungry, and almost exhausted when we got to Bad Wildbad.

Because we were such a small group of prisoners, we were able to bed down in what seemed like a typical American farmland country school house. This was a blessing in itself, but not the only one, because the vil*lagers* gave us some black bread and boiled potatoes, what was probably their regular diet during wartime. Even though it was about 9:00 p.m., a little girl gave me the food I received, and she seemed so sweet and innocent that every time I think about her it brings tears to my eyes. These vil*lagers* showed human kindness, and I realized that not all Germans were bad. The conditions actually reminded me of home because the country school that I had attended was very similar to this one. Our school had pictures of our endeared presidents, George Washington and Abraham Lincoln. Their school did not have any pictures of Hitler or any of his cohorts hanging on their walls. Clearly, not all the people under German command were avid Nazis. Our guards were part of the Wehrmacht and were not apparently under direct control of the SS, Hitler's personal forces sworn to protect their Fuhrer and to murder all those so ordered by him or the Gestapo. Our guards, unlike the SS, were decent soldiers in most instances and they permitted the villagers to help us as they did.

The next morning we continued walking easterly, thankful that we'd had some food the night before and had rested in a reasonably warm place. We were walking in the Black forest and the hills were steep but the scenery was simply beautiful. The forest was clean of underbrush and clear of dead limbs and was almost like a park, because the villagers used the dead brush for cooking and heating their homes. It was cold and miserable walking, but I thought about the times I had been on hikes with my dad under better circumstances and it helped me withstand the suffering by thinking about home. Toward nightfall on January 19, we stopped at some kind of forest camp and were fed a slice of bread and what I considered wonderful vegetable soup. God, did it ever hit the spot, and helped belay our hunger after two days with very little food. We had walked about 18 miles (29 km.) and were on the outskirts of Stuttgart. I learned after the war that we had been placed in a small temporary holding facility and not a regular camp but a temporary satellite of a major prisoner of war camp known as "Stalag VA" located at Ludwigs-burg, Germany, about nine miles (14 km.) north of Stuttgart.

We could tell we were in a temporary holding facility that was a gymnasium of sorts. There were no toilet or lavatory facilities available to us other than a slit trench in the open area outside the building and behind a barbed wire and cyclone type fencing that had been placed temporarily around the area. We were not transported to the larger camp, apparently because they planned on shipping us out of Stuttgart within two or three days without being registered as prisoners of war at Stalag VA.

We slept on the floor on lice-infested straw mats, but it was warm and our ration of food consisted of a loaf of bread for six men and a bowl each of cabbage soup. On the second day we received a handful of sugar with a slice of bread instead of the usual soup. I had no idea why, and the guards who brought the food had no comment as to why. Our small group had now become part of a larger group of enlisted men and officers that as yet had not been separated. This is where I met the colonel from the 79th division who with my captain was planning on trying to escape and who asked me to join them.

This was a short stay, and some of us had not as yet been thoroughly searched. I recall a few instances where some of us actually had paper money in various amounts that we used as toilet paper because none was ever provided to us and we wanted to avoid giving our money to the Germans. This got to be somewhat humorous, as though we soldiers had money to wipe and throw away, rather than burn.

One of the most serious events that occurred during my stay here was receiving a question from one of our senior officers who during the siege and battle at Herrlisheim had left his tank crew after giving orders to fight to the last man and then gone and hid in one of the buildings, leaving his men to fight and die. Fortunately two of them survived, but I did not know this or the circumstances of being left in the tank to fight to the last until after the war. They had not been taken prisoner with our group. This same officer as a prisoner, before we were separated, asked me, "Do you think that the Germans will kill us?" I said, "Yes, probably." He then started bawling and said, "I wish I was with my mother and had some of her chocolate cake." My conclusion was, "This is real officer material!" Enough said! Thank God for the enlisted men. I have not used names in this writing of my experiences, but believe me, I haven't forgotten any of them.

The second most serious event was that the night before being loaded on a train in the rail transport area of Stuttgart, we were shown a moving picture featuring Donald O'Conner in a song and dance routine. Afterwards the Germans explained to us that while we poor bastards were fighting and dying, people like O'Conner and his girlfriends and the other special people of the elite families in the United States were living the life of luxury.

My German was good enough to interpret this scenario. They did not speak to us totally in German but in a combination of broken English and German, trying to better explain what they meant, whereby they offered to correct the situation for us by giving us clean German uniforms, food, and cigarettes if we would sign up as German soldiers and go to fight the Russians, guaranteeing that we would later be protected from being charged with treason.

Their belief was that the soldiers of the British Commonwealth and the United States should unite and stop the great Bolshevik offensive that had now crossed the frontiers of Germany. They seemed to ignore the fact that they'd started the war with Russia under the code name "Barbarossa" on June 22, 1941.

At this point in time we were still in reasonably good physical condition and would have made good soldiers for them. Needless to say, they got no volunteers from our men. (See Appendix D for their total official proclamation recorded for posterity.)

By this point the bandage on my arm that had been placed on it while in the cellar at Herrilisheim was filthy and looked and smelled terrible. Fortunately, the initial sulfa powder that had been used had kept me from becoming badly infected. During the second day at this camp the German medics did change my bandage using white crepe paper, without any disinfectant, that they wrapped tightly around my arm. Their bandages were primarily made of non-colored crepe paper at this point during the war. Nothing further was used to limit possible infection, but luckily my arm continued to heal without additional medical treatment. We were at this temporary holding camp only three days, and then we were marched in a column of twos to the nearby Stuttgart railroad yards.

At the railroad we were loaded into box cars until there was standing room only, with no sanitary facilities other than an empty bucket that was filled within minutes and that only succeeded in taking up precious room, leaving us to stand in human waste with no means of wiping, washing, or cleaning ourselves. Unfortunately, there was no hole in the floor of the boxcar nor were we able to bust one through the bottom. When we relieved ourselves we had to use our hands, sometimes wiping them on our boots or pant legs. We were much like cattle that lie in their own bodily wastes that attach and dry in place.

We were confined in this manner for four and a half days without food or water to travel to the railroad center in Hannover, Germany, a distance of about 452 kilometers or 280 miles from Stuttgart. We traveled mostly at night and we were repeatedly strafed by friendly fire. The Allied aircraft pilots had no way of knowing what was in these hell cars. I believe that nearly every one of us had the G.I.'s, also known as the galloping trots, and it is impossible for anyone who was not there to realize what a hellhole this was or what the stench of human waste and the bodies of the dead, killed by the strafing, were like.

I don't how many died on the trip because being in a box car sealed without light made it impossible to see who was alive or dead or hardly anything else even during the daylight hours. In addition, we were almost all strangers to each other. Many of the dead were still standing, leaning against the living because of the confined space. There was a slight hole at my eye level in the side of the boxcar that allowed some light to come through where I was standing. This was a blessing later on because once while we were stopped on the tracks in a village during the night on a railroad spur, a displaced person or slave civilian Polish laborer who knew what was inside our boxcars climbed up on the side of the railroad car and passed through several tiny tin cans of water so that we could take turns wetting our lips and taking a few swallows. Considering the number of us in the boxcar, very few of us who were still alive had any chance of getting any water at all.

On the one hand this little amount of water was a blessing. On the other hand, I contracted acute intestinal amebiasis either from this water or later on in the prison camp. I was fortunate to live long enough to get back home and have this treated. When not successfully treated, the amoeba which is the cause of the infection can travel to the brain, causing death. This happened to one my fellow prisoners of war shortly after getting back home who, by the way, lived within 80 miles of my hometown. I visited his mother after I got home, and after her persistent requests, explained what the conditions were like in the camps and how I happened to know her son.

Our unknown friend in need had to leave after about 15 minutes because what he was doing was very dangerous and he had to avoid being seen by the train guards who walked up and down the train rails during the stops. The guards had no qualms about shooting anyone on sight if they were caught breaking the law or aiding the enemy. (There were many people like the Polish laborer who tried to help us and who were part of a large civilian slave labor force that existed throughout Germany.) As I learned later as a slave laborer myself, these individuals had limited freedom, whereas we had none, but they had to account for their actions and were required to report to their work or jobs on a regularly specified time basis. Although they were not under guard by military soldiers as we were, they had to have special papers and were subject to search at any time for verification. This was not only for security reasons, but because, as I learned through actual experience, a black market was flourishing. Although the SS were guilty of being part of a black market, they naturally did not want prisoners or slave laborers to benefit or to be a part of it.

This was the only water we received during the four and a half days we were in the railroad car. Of course, there was no food whatsoever. It is a known fact that it is difficult to survive much longer than about seven days without water.

During the day the train engineer tried to locate areas that would not be conspicuous to Allied aircraft while waiting for nightfall. Nonetheless, air raids destroyed a number of cars and an unknown number of the prisoners in them. We could hear the planes diving and strafing the train, followed by explosions of bombs and machine gun fire. Each time a plane made a pass, the bullets tore through parts of the roof of the boxcar and each time hit someone in the car. Fortunately for us, the bullets didn't kill us all and our car, although strafed several times, did not receive a direct hit from a bomb. How many were dead, we couldn't determine because of the sealed and darkened car. We couldn't even have a role call, because most of us were strangers to each other. We were like zombies. We didn't talk; we were only thinking of survival and of home and telling ourselves that in time this nightmare would have to end one way or another.

Finally, after what seemed like an endless journey, we stopped while it was still dark outside the car. We didn't know what time it was, but when they opened the doors of the boxcars a few civilians were congregated at the site. When we were ordered to disembark, those of us who were still alive did so, walking down a wooden ramp similar to what cattle use when being unloaded. As we limped down the ramp after being immobilized for so long, we heard the civilians holler at us, calling us "*Schwein!*" (which means "pigs" or "bastards") as though we were nothing better than animals, probably because of the stench that followed us and the way we looked. True enough, after that many days of confinement without food or water or sanitary facilities in a boxcar that normally should hold about 40 loaded to the point of standing room only with about 90 prisoners.

Regardless of the welcoming committee, it was nice to get out into the fresh air and away from the terrible stench in the cattle car. Those who were dead were left in the car and were picked up later by other less desirable sub-humans, by slave laborers, or by displaced citizens who were present in all the German cities. As I learned later, some of us were also to be so classified and did such clean-up work on a regular basis after bombing raids as part of the German war effort.

We were then marched from the train station in Fallingbostel, Germany, to Stalag X1 B, which was about two miles from the railroad train station. It was dark, and fortunately there weren't too many civilians along the way. I say fortunately, because at this time the civilian population had been subjected to so much incessant bombing that, given the chance, I am sure they would have tried to murder us like they attempted to do later during a work party where our guards had to protect us from their wrath. That occurrence took place during the following month after the Allied fire bombing of Dresden on February 13-14, 1945. The civilians were trying to kill us, and at that time we slave labor prisoners knew nothing about the fire bombing or the fact that 135,000 civilian people had lost their lives in a firestorm.

Even though the Allies did not bomb our area every night, the air raid sirens were going off as much as two to three times a night because of planes flying over us going somewhere in Germany on a bombing mission, and the civilian population and our guards had to heed each warning. This became a psychological nightmare to them as well as to us, although we knew the results would be of benefit to us.

As we arrived at the camp gates, we passed through a double wire fencing with barbed wire enclosure. The sections of barbed wire were about six inches apart and the space between the wire fences was about 10 or 12 feet, so that if you got through the first fence they could

49

still shoot you from a series of elevated guard towers that were spaced evenly along the barbed wire fencing that allowed overlapping machine gun fire.

After arriving at the camp, we were taken to a barracks that had wooden shelf-like bunks four tiers high with wooden slats. Some held straw or straw mats that were filthy, and it wasn't very long before I knew they were also filled with lice. Some of the bunks had nothing but the bare wooden slats.

After receiving instructions as to where and how we were to sleep, two to a bunk, we were each given a slice of black bread and a tin bowl of thin cabbage soup. We were to keep the tin bowl and carry it in our pants pockets. The cabbage soup was mostly hot water, and the black bread, I learned later, was made of flour and sawdust. The following is the recipe for black bread according to the records of the Food Providing Ministry:

50%   bruised rye grain
20%   sliced sugar beets
20%   tree flour (sawdust)
10%   minced leaves and straw

It was easy to lose weight on a diet such as this. The bread together with the watered down cabbage soup was enough to just barely keep you alive. As a matter of fact, now that they were losing the war, the German plan was to work and feed us this watered down cabbage soup with one slice of bread a day as a regular diet with the expectation that we would live and work about three months before dying.

This was our first food since our railroad trip had begun four and a half days before without heat in near zero temperatures. This was by no means very much food, but after being without food or heat for so long, it did help some. At least the watery soup was warm and it was also warm inside the barracks from the body heat of the prisoners. We were told we would be registered in the morning since we had arrived so late. At this time German manpower was critical because of the war, and that was the reason for allowing so many different nationalities of prisoners to remain alive and to work together until they died from exhaustion, starvation, and exposure.

Fallingbostel was a small village about 55 km. (34 miles) north of Hannover, Germany. The camp was divided into a number of individual barracks (or *lagers*) that separated the various nationalities, because of language differences, for sleeping and eating. Each *lager* had its own main entrance gate and held approximately 10 barracks buildings 40x130 feet, each holding about 250 men. In the middle of the barracks was a washroom with cold-water faucets. There were four sinks that had drain holes in the bottom, but no drain pipes. The wash water drained from the sink down to the concrete floor that was sloped to a hole over a septic tank below the floor, located in the center of the room. The toilet room was also a part of the washroom for use during the night.

The term "washroom" is used rather loosely because we never did have any soap, although the Russian and Polish prisoners we had contact with said that when someone we knew as a fellow *arbeiter* (worker) was missing, it was because he had died and his body was being burned and rendered for making soap. This was said while they pointed to the smoke stacks in the distance. We did not go by names very often, because of the language differences, but by recognizing faces and other features.

Outside the barracks, clearly visible to the guard towers, was the outdoor toilet consisting of two long poles mounted on each of the sides with an A-frame about eight feet apart that provided a place to sit in the open air over a large slit trench. The poles weren't any too high and it often was a problem to avoid spattering the poles or your pants. The poles were never clean and often were wet, slimy, and shitty. Later, at the slave labor camp, the toilets were of the same type but there were no inside toilets like those in Stalag XI B. At the slave labor camp it was extremely difficult to use the toilets at night because of darkness and the risk of being shot at the discretion of a guard while outside unless you were on your way to the open trench-type bomb shelter during an air raid.

Later on while at the slave labor holding facility, when the SS inspectors unexpectedly visited the camp, they would on occasion engage in the sport of shoving or pushing a prisoner off the poles into the toilet slit trench using a stick to avoid spattering their uniforms. (These types of toilet slit trenches were four to six feet deep while the general army type of slit trench was much shallower and only wide enough to permit a person to squat and straddle it.) Their primary purpose in engaging in such sport was to show their superiority towards us *unter-menschens*.

It had to take a great deal of effort to climb out of such filth, and try to imagine if you can what the circumstances were like in trying to clean up or remove the filth afterward when the only water supply for the camp was an outdoor faucet. I thank God, whom I believed in, although he was silent throughout the Holocaust, that this never happened to me. For those of you who read this, you may have a better understanding as to why very few ex-prisoners of war want to talk about their experiences. These comments are for my grandchildren and for those who I hope will see the brutality of some men during wartime and try to make a better world. The comments are also to dispute the revisionists who are claiming that none of these things really happened but were wartime propaganda.

The second night I was at Stalag XI B, before being sent to the slave labor holding facility, I got terribly sick during the night and I thought for sure I was going to die. I had terrible stomach cramps to the point where I was crawling around on the toilet room floor in agonizing pain, shitting and vomiting, trying to hit the toilet hole that was about a four-inch opening in the concrete floor directly over a cesspool. I was cold, wet, filthy, and burning up with fever. I often dreamed of this many years after the war. Toward morning I seemed to be somewhat better, and I cleaned myself up as much as I could, using the cold water faucet, and I got rid of most of the filth and stench. I was new to the camp and didn't know the routines, and I hadn't gotten acquainted with anyone yet, so I had to let my clothes dry in place on me and not take the chance of losing any of them. It was still winter and I had as yet no means of drying them without freezing. The cold helped reduce the stench.

The barracks buildings were made of plywood walls and roofs with wooden framing. The barracks buildings were elevated about two feet above the ground on concrete piers, making it impossible to construct any tunnels underneath without being observed by the guards. I was temporarily placed with some of the British soldiers who had originally been captured at Dunkirk, France, in 1940. I was there only a short time, but these men were fine soldiers. The name of one of these soldiers has stuck with me, "Brigham Young." This was an easy one to remember because of my school history lessons of the Brigham Young who founded the church in Utah. I later received an honorary medal from the British government for being with the British soldiers in that camp.

The next morning a German corporal came through the barracks, yelling, "*Aufstehen!*" ("Get up!") He then directed us to fall out and line up for roll call (*zahlappell*). We went outside, lined up, and he began counting. After roll call, we went back in the barracks, and a cart with *ersatz* (coffee) came in and each of us was given a tin bowl of so-called coffee. The *ersatz* was apparently made from some type of ground roasted bean. It didn't taste much like coffee, but it did have some nourishment. We also received a slice of black bread, and that was it for breakfast. Later on at the labor camp we generally got only the *ersatz* in the morning and cabbage soup and a slice of black bread at night. We were then ordered outside and told to line up to go to registration. We walked over to another wooden building and were ordered inside. There, we lined up in front of a table and a German sergeant with the assistance of an American prisoner asked a series of questions.

The American, prior to being under the scrutiny of the German sergeant, advised us to list our religion as Protestant and to have been farmers before the war. We were asked our name, rank, and serial number, religion, home address, branch of service, unit, if we had been wounded, and what we did before the war. That last question was easy for me since I was still in school when I left for the army. Being a student prior to the war was also a good answer. They also wanted our dog tags, in order to check our serial numbers and religion. I did not have my dog tags; I had lost them either while diving out of my tank or while crawling towards the tank at my rear, or later while trying to shoot the German infantry bastards who were gunning for us.

I knew from the comments the night before from prisoners who were already in camp that they would be looking for Jewish soldiers and would be checking dog tags for the letter "H" for Hebrew. As mentioned earlier, some of those with Jewish-sounding names were also checked to see if they had been circumcised. Those who were suspected of being Jewish or who had Jewish names were separated and sent to separate *lagers* after the registration and were to be part of what I learned later was the "Final Solution." As I said before, I was apparently suspected of being Jewish or was considered a misfit, for I was sent to a slave labor holding facility, and I learned later what that was to mean. I was given a wooden dog tag with the number 135085, and fortunately I was allowed to keep my field jacket and my boots.

During the registration, believe it or not, they took the boots from some of us and replaced them with open-toed wooden shoes with canvas straps that caused unbelievable suffering while working outside in the snow during the rest of the winter with only body heat at night in the camp that we were in. Remember, this was still winter, in one of the coldest winters on record. I believe that the only reason they didn't take my boots was because of the size of my feet or that the tops were filthy from the conditions in the boxcar and my sickness in the toilet. We did not take our boots off at night for fear of having them stolen.

It is interesting to note that my field jacket, like many of the others, was not taken. A generally unknown fact that the German soldiers conveyed to me later was that when they saw our infantry coming with the field jacket hoods over their steel helmets, many of them imagined that the face they saw within the shadowed hood was the face of a death skull, and many of them were unusually fearful.

Stalag X1 B was originally a training camp large enough to train a full German division for Hitler's new army. After the invasion of Poland it became a prisoner of war camp filled with Polish soldiers captured in September of 1939. After the German invasions of France, Belgium, the Netherlands, and Russia, the camp became a working prisoner-of-war camp for French, Belgian, Dutch, Jewish, British, Russian, Czechoslovakian, Italian, and American prisoners of war. By mid 1944, the number of prisoners was over 96,000. As a working prisoner-of-war camp, the internees were formed into *arbeitskommandos* (working commands) and sent out to farms, factories, villages, and the city of Hannover. When we arrived in February of 1945, the camp was in a terrible state. The lack of food and medical supplies were causing all kinds of problems, including death caused by outbreaks of typhus.

On Friday, February 2, 1945, the Americans in the barracks at Stalag XI B were ordered outside, lined up, and roll call was taken. While in line, a corporal walked through the lineup and picked 12 of us, including me, and directed us to follow him. Since no registration information was used to select us, I believe the guards may have gotten suggestions from cooperating Americans as to who might be Jewish or a troublemaker. The remaining American prisoners of war stayed in the legally designated Stalag XI B as prisoners, not slave laborers, until they were liberated.

My group of 12 was led to what had been a school bus painted a dark green and directed to enter. We did, and we were driven to Hannover under guard, a distance of about 34 miles or 55 km., directly to a diesel refining plant, and ordered to disembark. We got off the bus and right then and there we knew we were in real trouble.

The first thing we saw was an SS guard with a large black horsewhip striking some poor bastard who was standing up in the diked area surrounding a fuel storage tank in water and fuel that was waist deep, trying to repair a shrapnel leak from a previous bombing by plugging it with a gasket-type insert. The leak in the tank was above the surface of the water and fuel mix, and the water had collected in the diked area along with the fuel that had leaked out.

I don't know what the temperature was, but it was cold and ice had been forming on the surface of the water areas, and he had to work in conditions like this without heat or any means of drying his clothes after completing the repair job. I learned that this was to be expected in a slave labor camp, so that if you weren't starved to death you also had the daily opportunity to die from bombing, exposure, or being shot by a visiting SS guard or by one of our own Wehrmacht guards for that matter if they chose to do so.

We were introduced to a German civilian foreman who was responsible for directing us to the work that was expected of us. We had two regular Wehrmacht guards who were not part of the SS group and who had served on the Russian Front and had been wounded and classified as limited service. One guard we called Hans had his left hand and part of his arm blown off, but he could still use his right hand and the prosthesis on his left arm to carry and shoot his rifle when necessary. The other guard we called Krank (sick) because he limped and looked sickly. He apparently had been wounded in the legs or hips while also at the Russian Front. The civilian foremen we called Pinocchio for obvious reasons. He had one of the longest noses of anyone I had ever seen.

Our first job was to clean the mortar off the bricks that had previously been used to protect the fuel tanks from bombings. The expression was *"commen mit der messers."* A steel knifelike blade was used to knock the mortar off the brick. We had quotas with the threat of "or else." This wasn't the only clean-up job we had, but we did enough to learn how to beat the quota system. We would wheel the cleaned bricks to an area and dump them where they were counted. Pinocchio would count them, and if we had enough to satisfy him nothing further was said. We learned that by distracting him we could sneak back, in a roundabout way, some of the cleaned bricks to our work area, and re-submit them for a count. This worked rather well. He apparently did not catch on. If he did, he never said anything.

The bricks when cleaned were wheeled to civilian forced laborers who by trade were masons. The masons laid up the protective brick walls surrounding the tanks in the diked areas to protect the tanks from shrapnel during bombing raids. A diked area is the area surrounding a fuel tank and consists of an earthern berm high enough to contain the fuel within the tank if and when the tank springs a leak from an explosion or shrapnel. The intent, as a safety measure, is for the diked area to hold the fuel rather than have it run over the ground and be unrecoverable.

While we were engaged in this type of work we were surprised one day by a civilian worker who spoke excellent English and who we found out was from Brooklyn, New York. As an American, he was in Hannover prior to the war as a technician for Standard Oil Company. Connected with the initial plant refining process, he was unable to leave Germany after the war started. We didn't have many conversations with him and he kept his distance from us, probably because of his orders. He may have been a sympathetic German as well.

There were some benefits to working in the refining plant. We could get warm at times from the heat from some of the pipes that transported hot water, and we were also able to get paraffin from some of the plants by scraping it from the vats. This we took and used as candles and to warm our hands back at camp.

Our guards, Hans and Krank and Pinocchio, were decent people and often expressed to us, *"Alles kaput"* ("Everything is finished"). They seemed certain that the war was lost and appeared to believe there was no reason to treat us like the SS had instructed them. The SS, by the way, checked us out periodically and had no qualms about beating us with their rifle butts or clubs to show their superiority as part of their master race. They often screamed at the guards for being what they called too lax.

On occasion we were able to supplement our meager food supply by taking advantage of our guards, who probably were not the brightest German soldiers. As an example, while working in the diesel fuel refining plant, we found out that the two guards kept their lunch in a tool shed. When we had the opportunity to slip into the tool shed, we took only one of the lunches, the theory being that one of the guards would blame the other for stealing his lunch. Believe it or not, this worked several times and the guards were hostile with each other, accusing each other of stealing their lunch. Neither guard suspected any of us. They apparently believed that if it was one of us stealing a lunch, we would have taken both of them. Because we were starving, it was indeed very hard to keep from taking both lunches.

Our daily routine was the same. Each morning a guard came into our barracks yelling *"Aufstehen!"* at about 4:00 a.m. I say "about" 4:00 a.m. because none of our small group had a timepiece or a watch. Our watches had all been taken from us. We worked until dark, and if we asked the guards or Pinocchio, *"Wieviel uhr ist es?"* ("What's the time?"), they answered, *"Vas macht das aus?"* ("What difference does it make?")

We lined up and were counted. Since we were such a small group, it was a quick process. We then got our daily tin cup of what they called coffee, and that was all until dark, after we walked back to our barracks. We didn't receive our daily slice of black bread and our tin cup of cabbage soup until returning from work at night. It wasn't long before the loss of weight and our loss of strength began to show significantly. After roll call we were marched off to the refining plant or to some other location in the city to spend the day cleaning bricks or rubble caused by the periodic bombing by the Allies.

CHAPTER 5

Life in a Slave Labor Camp

During the daily routine of clean-up work, often in the city of Hannover cleaning up rubble and debris from bombings, we were subjected to air raids or warnings day and night. Although we weren't bombed daily, we were nevertheless forced to seek shelter along with the guards in air raid trenches that offered some protection from shrapnel. On a few occasions I happened to be in the right clean-up area and was permitted to seek protection in a civilian bomb shelter along with our guards, though this depended on where we were when the air raid siren went off. On one occasion, while on my way to a civilian bomb shelter, the guards as usual were ahead of me, running for the shelter, when a women, panic-stricken, looking for one of her children, handed me a sack of potatoes (*kartoffels*) and asked me to hold them while she looked for her child.

Needless to say, she did not recognize me as a *kriegsgefangene*. I did not have the usual "KG" lettered on the back of my jacket and we were often mixed with civilians during air raids. Anyway, I disappeared quickly with the potatoes and she did not recover them. I shared them with my colleagues and we were able to eat them later, raw, because at this camp we had no way of doing any cooking other than by using a candle in an attempt to roast them.

This was the last time I was near this bomb shelter, and shortly after this incident, the shelter experienced a direct hit and was destroyed. From then on we had to go to an open area that was sur-rounded by berms and mounds of excavated earth that had been used in constructing a railroad grade surrounding the area. This shelter felt somewhat like being in a valley, and though it did not offer much protec-tion from air raids, it was not a specific bombing target and was better than nothing.

Before the bombing got excessive, during the end of February, we always walked to our work area from our barracks at about 4:00 a.m., and after reaching the downtown area of Hannover, we were sometimes put on a street car with a guard at each end to ride across the city to do clean-up work from previous bombings. Since we often were in groups of 6 to 12 assigned to such tasks, we were at times with German civilian workers while on the streetcar. One day I managed to relieve one of the workers of his lunch that he had placed on the overhead rack while I was walking off the streetcar. This was a dangerous move considering the fact that the guards could have shot me for such stealing, especially for stealing food, which was in critical supply at this stage of the war.

I learned sometime later that most of the German civilian workers carried their lunches in briefcases that they held tightly under their arms. I assume they did not want to take a chance of losing their lunches because food sources were extremely critical even for civilians. Their lunches usually consisted of a slice of black bread, sometimes covered with margarine, and some small boiled potatoes with the skins still on them.

By the beginning of March the streetcar lines had been destroyed by bombs, along with most of the water and sewer lines within the city. Many of the streetcar rails were sticking up vertically in the air along with huge piles of earthen mounds and craters as a result of the bombings. These craters, and there were lots of them, were useful while working in the diesel refining plant or in other areas of the city because we used them as latrines when necessary since they were at every work site. They were generally also partly filled with water, and since we didn't have any form of toilet paper, the water in the craters helped us clean our hands and our rear ends. After the streetcars were destroyed, we generally walked to and from whatever work area we had to clean up.

A few times six of us were taken to various areas of downtown Hannover by truck. This was not unusual except for the fact that the truck was run by a coal burner mounted directly in back of the cab on the driver's side. Just how this worked, I was unable to exactly figure out, but it appeared there were two compartments for the coal. One compartment had coal above a lower container that was burning coal, and the other container above the burning coal was non-burning but was heated to the point that the gas in the non-burning coal container was driven off. This was probably methanol, which was piped to the engine pistons, where it was fired and drove the engine. The Germans were known to have this type of technology in the 1940s. They appeared to have several such trucks, which moved slowly but were effective.

The distance from our so-called barracks or holding area was about two to four miles, depending upon where we went to do clean-up work. We did not work at the refining plant every day; that was about a four-mile walk from our holding facility. On one of our routes we passed a couple of trailers that housed Polish prostitutes for the benefit of the German soldiers. I am sure the girls had been imported from Poland and were forced into this profession. We were unable to determine just what German military forces had the opportunity to visit them, but it was an established location for that specific purpose. It was apparent to us that our guards were familiar with the operation. During an air raid when our guards headed for the air raid shelter ahead of us, as they often did, a couple of the prostitutes came out. In spite of the ongoing air raid siren, they asked if we had any cigarettes or chocolate as trade items. Of course none of us had any cigarettes or chocolate, and if we did, we had only one thing on our mind, and that was food not sex. We thought about food continuously, and imagined all the ways we could get, cook, and eat food. Nothing else mattered; we were starving and all we thought about day and night was food.

I mentioned the fact that our guards often were ahead of us during an air raid when we were headed for a shelter. The question arises, why didn't we take the opportunity to escape? The answer is that during this time, everything was chaotic, and German soldiers as well as prisoners of war had to have travel papers regardless of conditions. If stopped by the SS troops who seemed to be everywhere attempting to maintain law and order, you had to produce satisfactory papers. If you didn't, you were tried on the spot, so to speak, and shot or hung at the site. There was substantial evidence of this being done by the number of photographs that were found after the war that had been taken of such hangings directly from street lampposts and the dead bodies lying in the streets. This chaotic condition existed because a number of German soldiers were deserting daily and did not have proper papers, as well as prisoners of war and slave laborers who were bent on escaping. The SS troops wanted to instill terrible fear in all potential German soldier deserters, prisoners of war, and slave civilian laborers to prevent such things from happening.

We were able, on rare occasions, to supplement our food supply while at work thanks to help from the civilian forced laborers and from some of the Polish workers who had been prisoners. Poland had surrendered in 1939, and these Polish workers had been able to establish some black market connections after having been part of the designated *arbeitskommandos*. The black market was primarily engaged in acquiring ration coupons that were more valuable than money. These coupons were little blue ration stamps much like the label on American Prince Albert tobacco cans. With one of these coupons and the right connections with the civilian forced laborers, it was possible on rare occasions to get a loaf of black bread without any money. Money had less value than the ration coupons or American cigarettes, which were quite valuable as a trade commodity.

Although we were under guard at all times, except during air raids, we did have the opportunity to work with and trade with civilian forced laborers without being caught by our guards. Without a doubt, that helped keep us alive. Our group owed a great deal to these Polish workers like

Bejec Woichevski, who was doing the same type of clean-up work we were. We could communicate with each other because, like me, he also spoke some German. These forced laborers helped us without getting anything in return. On one occasion I had been given one of these little blue ration coupons from Bejec as a gift for future trading, and I placed it in my watch pocket for future use when the opportunity arose.

Being caught by the SS with this type of coupon or any other black market evidence as a prisoner of war at this stage of the war meant death without trial and at the discretion of the SS since they had such automatic powers. The SS had a habit of arriving unexpectedly from the four main directions all at once and then conducting a search for contraband items such as ration stamps. When I had been given such coupons by Bejec or others who had black market connections with forced slave civilian laborers, I generally placed them in my right boot. The reason for the right boot was that when the SS searched us they always told us to take off our left boot to look for such coupons. That must have been the instructed procedure in their training manuals. On this occasion I still had a coupon in my watch pocket. On this particular day, the SS swooped in on us while we were working and began their search. The SS soldier who was searching me reached into my watch pocket and palmed the coupon without comment and continued searching me, including my left boot, the traditional method. The SS soldier who found and palmed my coupon was a young soldier and he had the authority to dispatch me on site. The only reason I believe he did not do so was that he, like many others, was becoming sick of so much killing.

By the middle of March, 1945, I had lost nearly one hundred pounds. Though I was emaciated, I still had my dull razor, and having been instilled with the thinking of General Patton and the importance of not only being a soldier but also looking like one, I kept shaven as best as I could using cold water from bomb craters and from the one faucet we had available at our holding facility. I kept my razor reasonably sharp by rubbing the blade on my belt. The bombing had increased in intensity, and we had to run to the trench shelter two and three times a night as well as during the day. The Germans had placed an 88 mm. anti-aircraft gun right near our quarters and this did not help, because our building was not marked as a prisoner of war building. Fortunately, we were not hit directly. These days became more hectic than ever, and the guard we called Hans disappeared; he may have deserted. He was replaced by a likeable old chap who had or was raising six kids. He was apparently from the Volkstrum and lived in a neighboring area close to our camp. He often told us that Germany had been out of control for some time and, like our other guards, that *"Alles kaput."* This became a common expression of the German people.

On Easter Day, March 29, 1945, it was cold and snowy and we were marched to work as always, but the general attitude of our guards conveyed a feeling of uneasiness. We also learned from our civilian slave labor contacts that the Allies were apparently getting close to Hannover. I could tell the guards were uneasy. Two days later we were not ordered to march to work, but remained in the barbed wire area outdoors after roll call. Why, we didn't know, but while milling around we saw a German soldier with a captured American soldier who had an armored division patch on his left arm. They were taking him into their headquarters building nearby, which was part of our holding facility. We yelled, "What outfit are you with?" and "How far are you away from here?"

He replied "6th Armored and about 10 miles from here." We were happy to hear this, but because he answered, the soldier guarding him hit him in the head with his rifle butt, knocking him down. He was bleeding badly, but he got up after being kicked and went into the building. We didn't see any more of him, but we knew it wouldn't be long before we'd be out of this hellhole.

By April 3, 1945, the bombing raids were becoming intense and it seemed that we were spending most of our time in the trench shelters or the bermed area near where we were working. The lack of sleep because of the continuous sirens warning of impending bombers and the lack of food were really taking a toll now; we were all becoming weaker and weaker and were having a difficult time walking, let alone working. The comment of the day by the civilian foreman was, *"Ihr schdweinehunde"* ("You bastards)", *"wenn ich euch sage was ihr tun sollt outwortet ihr immer, ich verstehe nicht"* ("when I tell you to do something, you always respond by saying, 'No, I don't understand'"), *"aber wenn ich sage es ist fierabend dann versteht ihr jedes wort"* ("but when it's time to quit work you understand every word").

During these last days, while heading for the bermed bomb shelter, we noticed that one of the diesel fuel tanks had sprung a leak and there was a considerable accumulation of oil in the bermed area. So in passing, with the guards as usual ahead of us, we were able to torch off the oil. Fortunately we were not observed, and a hell of a fire ensued. This was not the first such incident. On one other occasion we noticed a German soldier standing on the other side of a masonry wall that was part of the rubble of a building left over from a bombing. We were able to push it over on him. We don't know whether or not he survived and we didn't hang around to find out, because at this time the Volkstrum were active and carried various weapons with orders to shoot to kill anyone caught committing such crimes. We knew that we were near the end of our imprisonment, but we were not sure just how long it would be before we were liberated. We knew that the American and British troops were very close.

On April 11, 1945, we were told that we would not be going to work as usual but were to begin a march to Hamburg. While we were waiting to begin the march, our regular guards were replaced with SS along with one of their officers, so we knew our treatment during the march would not be pleasant. We were lined up in twos and left the compound and began our march to Hamburg. We didn't have to pack for damn sure, because all we had were the clothes on our backs and the tin bowls we were given originally. We started with anticipation, because we knew it wouldn't be long before we would be liberated. Our first day we walked about halfway to Celle, Germany, about 19 miles (30 km.) northeasterly from Hannover. During our march there were two notable events. The first was that we were straffed by Allied aircraft that apparently thought we were the enemy. We ran to the side of the road and hit the ground, and fortunately this time there were forests on each side of the roadway. Incredible as it may seem, I was lucky again, because during the strafing a scared rabbit started running alongside of me in the trees and was hit by bullets but was able to still run, although crippled and bleeding.

After the strafing, the second somewhat humorous event was that during our march that day, a column of Ukrainians from another camp marching directly in front of us encountered a chicken from a nearby farm that started to run across the road. The chicken never made it to the other side. The only sound as the chicken reached the marching soldiers was a suppressed gurgle. Not one of the Ukrainians missed a step, and then we observed one feather, then another, and so on with internal pieces of the chicken being dropped little by little. The Ukrainians cleaned and cut up the chicken without missing a step, and I assume they shared it as a food supplement with one another later on. It went so smoothly that their guards were totally oblivious to the whole event.

One of the most degrading things that happened to us during our march towards Hamburg was that when we had to defecate, we were instructed by our guards to run ahead so that we were still in view of the guards and prisoners behind us, who were walking at a normal pace. In front of them all, we had to relieve ourselves and rinse our hands in a roadside puddle, if available. If we took too long and visibility on behalf of the guards could not be maintained before we could get back in formation, we were to be shot. We were not able to choose when and where we defecated, because we were all suffering from the galloping trots almost all the time and not from overeating.

Food was a prime commodity at this time in our lives. There was no question that we were starving to death. As a matter of fact, while we were billeted in the farm the first night of our march toward Hamburg, I ate some raw oats that were in the barn and I will never forget the raw husks being caught in my throat. I also ate what I believe were raw sugar beets, what the Germans referred to as cow beets. At any rate they made me sicker than a dog that first night on the road. We also ate dandelion leaves and at one stop near an oak tree I ate some raw acorns. They were bitter, but they did have some nutritive value.

CHAPTER 6

Liberation by the 15th Scottish Division

O n April 12, 1945, towards evening, we were northwest of Celle, Germany, when I noticed that our camp comman- dant who had the markings of an SS officer and who had also replaced our regular guards with SS guards on our march to Hamburg had changed into civilian clothes and was riding away on a bicycle. There was no doubt in my mind that he was well aware that the SS in general had violated all of the conditions of the Geneva Convention. He was leaving our guards behind, and I knew then that the Allies were nearby. The following morning on Sunday, April 13, 1945, the 15th Scottish Division liberated us.

This was a wonderful experience for us and one that I shall always remember. They gave us some food as best they could and also de-loused us. They gave me part of a British uniform and a knapsack to carry along with some new boots. My clothes were burned in the middle of the street, and I swear I could see them moving because of the lice infestation being subjected to the fire. The British/Scottish made temporary plumbing arrangements so that we could finally wash with hot water before putting on our clean clothes. What a relief, especially to those who could smell us after more than four months without a bath since Strasbourg. After this brief interlude, I was actually afraid of the possibility of a German counterattack, and I decided right then and there that I was going to haul ass toward the rear, which I did. I caught a ride on a truck transport.

On the way the truck stopped temporarily at a campground that had been used by the Allied troops and I found some crusts of bread lying on the ground. I grabbed them without hesitation because I was still hungry and I had a subconscious fear of not wasting or seeing any type of food being wasted. I still have that fear today.

The transport truck was headed back towards Celle, and while riding we were informed that President Roosevelt had died the day before on April 12, 1945. This was sad news for all of us. We knew how much we and the world owed this man and why we had to fight the war, especially after witnessing firsthand the horrible atrocities of the Nazis. To my mind, it was sad he hadn't lived to see the end of the war and all the results of the Holocaust.

When we got to Celle, we were informed that a rehabilitation center was being formed at the castle formerly owned by King George of Hannover. We were directed to go there and register as American ex-prisoners of war. We were to be brought up to date and to start planning our return to the United States. As we got near the castle we came across some of the Red Cross trailers that had coffee, cigarettes, doughnuts, milk, and other goodies. All we needed was money. As a reader of this, you know damn well there was no way in hell we had any money coming out of a Nazi concentration camp. In spite of viewing all the goodies such as milk and ice cream, we had to move on to the rehabilitation center as hungry as ever. You will also understand that I have not nor will I ever make a donation to the Red Cross at any time during the rest of my life. Enough said with emphasis!

We were billeted temporarily in the quarters of the former King George of Hannover along with many Russians, British, and American ex-prisoners of war. It was wonderful, and I did sleep in a four-poster bed in a bedroom with all the golden colored ornate trim, beautiful rugs, furniture, and paintings.

Life was beginning all over again for me. As ex-prisoners wandering around the castle, we found many riches stashed in the basement and throughout the castle. There were beautiful paintings, works of art, silverware, expensive furnishings, and all sorts of expensive items stored in the basement. Unfortunately, we could not carry it off as loot. We had been warned by the military police that all such things were off limits to us. The main thing for us was to get back to civilization so to speak, which we did.

I had a mixed bag with regards to my clothing. I had part of a British uniform, part of a Polish uniform, and was wearing a pair of German officer's boots that the former owner no longer needed. I was able to take them home but very little else as souvenirs. I was near Brussels, Belgium, wearing my combination uniform, and since I apparently looked so unusual, a young reporter singled me out for an interview. I found out later from the printed press release that it was Walter Cronkite, long before he became a notable news reporter and recognized as a notable foreign correspondent. He was covering the general area and was interviewing some of the ex-prisoners of war. He sent a press release that got to my hometown paper, stating that I had been held for a short time in East Prussia and was on my way home.

In a way, I was very glad he interviewed me because my folks still had no idea I was alive. As a matter of fact, my mother, who had been divorced from my dad, had received separately a previous telegram saying I had been killed in action, perhaps because my dog tags had been found that I'd lost in Herrllisheim, France.

I had been given the opportunity by the Red Cross to send a telegram notifying my parents that I was alive and would be home soon. Like the no-money episode with the Red Cross when I first got out of the prisoner of war camp, the telegram never got to my parents. In any event, I was free to head for the coast as I saw fit. We all were still emaciated and not in the best of health, and the army was very considerate of our condition and our feelings. Our ultimate goal was to get to Camp

Lucky Strike on the French coast at LeHavre. From there, we were to be loaded on a ship and sail for home.

While still at King George's castle, one of the primary concerns continued to be food. One time I was with a group of Russians and one of their main interests was making soup. They proceeded to grab everything they could and built fires outside the castle and began cooking whatever they could to make soup. On one occasion, unable to read or understand German, they dumped louse powder in the soup for flavoring. They were a raucous bunch but great people, and most of them seemed to have no ill effects from such food combinations. However, there was a sad experience when one of the Russian troops mistakenly ate a number 10 can of dehydrated potatoes he had gotten from the army kitchen, not realizing what happens when water or the liquid in the stomach comes into contact with the dehydrated contents. He was in critical condition and having a difficult time breathing when I last saw him and was near death. He had bloated so badly from the dehydrated potatoes and their absorption of water and his stomach liquids that he looked like he was about to have a baby.

Whenever we asked the Russians, *"Kak poshaviete?"* ("How are you?"), they always responded, *"Ochen horoshaw spasiebo"* ("Very well, thank you"). I did get to speak fairly good Russian from my contact with Bejec, but their alphabet is cryllic and is difficult to translate into English using the English alphabet.

Before we left the rehabilitation center, the British paymaster gave us each a month's pay so we could buy some of the necessaries we might need as we headed for the coast and Camp Lucky Strike. This payment was never charged against our account as U.S. soldiers. I was most appreciative of the splendid treatment we received from the 15th Scottish Division and the British government, and I shall never forget it.

We didn't have any restrictions, so I headed for the coast, hitchhiking, and I even got a free train ride to Paris. I managed to drink a few beers in Paris and enjoyed myself immensely. From there, I hitched an army air transport C47 to Brussels, Belgium. While in Brussels, I collapsed on the street from the ill effects of being a prisoner, and apparently the police picked me up. They knew I was an American soldier and they put me in the hospital. At that time my stomach was not yet used to food. We had to eat very little at a time and ingest it gradually; otherwise we would get terribly sick. They kept me there for about 10 days, taking care of me until I could continue my journey towards the French coast. They were simply wonderful to me, and they didn't ask for nor did they expect me to pay for such hospitality. When I got out they suggested I go to the British Embassy in Brussels and perhaps meet some other Americans. I did find the building, and after entering I was invited to have tea, by Sarah Churchill no less, who was visiting the embassy at the time. This was also a once-in-a-lifetime experience.

During the last week of April, 1945, I ran into some other GIs who were also headed for Camp Lucky Strike. After we had registered and the army had acknowledged that we'd survived and were no longer missing in action, we filled out various report forms for notifying our families and were given papers of identification. Since army transports were continually traveling to the coast, we could leave as we chose, at least that was my understanding and was what I did. While in Belgium, several restaurants gave me free meals without asking because they had a great deal of respect for American soldiers.

I was more or less planning on hitchhiking when I ran into a pair of GIs who had been prisoners of war. As they'd moved westward towards the coast, they had managed to steal an automobile and were riding in style. I didn't join them, although they did extend an invitation. They had been making their journey quite profitable, because while crossing Germany they would periodically stop and ask *"Wie spat ist es?"* ("What time is it?") Then when the German took out his watch, they relieved him of it. They had accumulated a bag of watches and planned on selling them when they got near the camp in order to take the money home. I don't know how much they got for the watches, because I didn't stay with them, but more than likely from the number of watches they had, it was a fairly good sum. I assume they also sold the automobile. This was their way of getting back at the Germans.

Our tank crew was guilty of something similar when we were in France during a lull in the fighting. It seems that this Frenchmen told us that he had several cases of champagne that he could use as trade. Our sergeant suggested that he might be able to make a deal, and trade a jeep for six cases of champagne. The Frenchman agreed and the exchange was made. Two days later he came back with an MP who had re-possessed the jeep and he was waving his arms in the air and pointing in all directions, trying to identify who had made the trade. Of course, this was one case where we all looked alike, and the evidence hadn't lasted long at all. Ah, oui, oui, the spoils of war. My conscience didn't bother me, and the champagne was welcome indeed.

I finally made it to LeHavre and Camp Lucky Strike. We got our papers, orders, and instructions and were ready to sail. On May 1, 1945, we were loaded on the hospital ship USS *George Washington* and set sail for home. We were in the middle of the Atlantic Ocean when we heard that the Germans had surrendered on May 8, 1945. I was on my way home, and what happened from then on is another story.

APPENDIX A

Comments

by Robert J. Hartwig,
C Company, 134th Ordinance Battalion,
12th Armored Division

L ate last night we moved into a town, a very new town in the sense that the Krauts had just run out of it. That is, most of them. Even though it was late, we roamed around a little, catching all the late rumors. During our wandering we came across an American first sergeant and a British officer who had been released that day from a German prison camp. They told us some of the atrocities practiced by the Germans on their prisoners. We took their stories, as one might say, with a grain of salt and didn't fully believe all they had to say. They told us of slowly being starved, of having to eat snails, dandelions, and weeds, and occasionally some very thin potato soup.

Later in the evening at a meeting, our captain told us of a slave labor camp near us where it was believed some 200 people had been burned that morning. That seemed as impossible to us as did the other stories. The next morning I had a chance to ride to this scene, to actually view the results of mass barbarianism, and to take some pictures. The party consisted of Captain Jones, Corporal Tannehill, the driver, Private First Class Singer, the interpreter, and myself. After driving about eight miles we became conscious of the sickening odor of burning bodies. About a mile to our right were some smoking ruins. We drove past both American and German signs warning of typhus.

As we rode toward the buildings the sight that met our eyes seemed unbelievable. There were rows upon rows of dead – dead who had died many horrible deaths. We learned that the majority of them had been given injections. Injections of what we could not be sure, some were poisoned and others were killed by an injection of oxygen into their bloodstreams. We know that some of them were as long as 30 hours dying. Even when we were there an occasional groan could be heard from someone dying in that mass or a movement of an arm or leg could be seen. The expressions on their faces were indescribable, as were the positions they were in, some half sitting, others up on one arm or in a twisted grotesque shape.

For now let us identify the place as the Landsburg Concentration Camp Area. In the short time we were there we drove by several separate camp sites, each occupying possibly a thousand acres, one of which we explored rather thoroughly. This one was know as the *krankenlager*, meaning in English "the sick camp." It was where the biggest burnings took place. Many buildings were left standing, some of which we went through. The odor was nauseating. The floor of each building was of dirt and dug about three feet below the surface of the ground. Each had a roughly constructed wooden roof covered with dirt. There was no provision for drainage and the slightest rain would leave water on the floor. Each building was about 50 feet long by 15 feet wide, with a shelf two feet high and five feet wide along each wall. A small pad of straw was the bedding, if any, for the prisoners sleeping on the shelf. They slept with their feet toward the middle of the aisle, either partly doubled up or their feet hanging over the end. There was usually one stove in the middle of each building, without fuel. I am sure there wasn't as much fuel in the whole camp as I have seen behind the average farmhouse in Germany. There was one small window at each end.

The Germans claimed the condition of the prisoners was due to typhus. We know this was not true. Their ill health was due to malnutrition, misuse, and overwork. The kitchen was a filthy, half-open building and contained large cooking pots used to prepare soup and liquid foods. There was nothing in the building that could have been used for preparing solid foods of any kind. Their food ration consisted of potato soup made to proportions of one pound of potatoes to one gallon of water. To make it worse, the cooks ate considerable of the potatoes instead of using them in the soup. One, one-pound loaf of bread was usually issued for eight men each day.

The standard uniform for this camp was a gray and black vertically striped pajama-like suit. The suit was of thin cotton flannel. There was no underclothing. We counted about one blanket for each 10 men. A doctor visited the camp about every two days – not for treatment but to send back to work any who might be able to work, even a little.

Much of our information was gathered from two living inmates who had escaped a few days before into the woods. They had guessed from the actions of the guards that the Americans were coming. One of these fellows was a Russian and another was Jewish. They told us that approximately 400 in walking condition were marched away the day before the Americans came. About 4,000 had been put in the camp originally. We saw the records kept in the camp. All of the people here were political prisoners. About three-fourths of them were Jewish and the rest a mixture of other races. The Jewish fellow had watched his wife and children be put in the gas chamber at a nearby camp. He had been used on the same work detail that had cleaned those bodies of his family out of the chamber when dead. He explained to us a common method of death there before the gas chamber was erected. A pit about 9x30 feet was filled with burning coals and live humans were poured into it from railroad dump-cars. The ashes were used for fertilizer.

The first pile of dead contained about 500 bodies. Some were burnt, many were given injections, and many more were beaten to death. Others were chopped with an axe; they were all freshly dead with the bodies still warm and soft. The skin was waxy and wrapped tight around the bones. The largest average diameter of their thighs was less than five inches. The hands were like claws. The skin was worn through to the meat on the hands and knees of those who couldn't walk, only could crawl. Many carried open wounds – old wounds for there was not nutrition to repair the tissues. Arms and legs were broken, hanging, rotting.

The GIs went to town that morning. They collected about 200 Nazi citizens and marched them out to the camp. They were real nice Germans – the wealthy ones, and let me say I don't believe one has money here unless he is a Nazi. Out at camp they were divided into two groups. Part of them were put to digging mass graves. Each grave was about 30x15 feet; there were rows of them. GIs were in charge – the digging didn't stop, nor was there any hesitation on the part of the diggers. Rifle butts and bayonets were law. Here let me speak of the released Russian who had the run of the place. He was one of the busiest persons I have ever seen. His working tool was similar to a ball bat. He just wandered back and forth among the civilians, picking out the slackers. Occasionally he took time out to talk to us.

Other groups of civilians were paired off and marched to outer areas, some more than a mile away, to pick up more dead. Two carried one dead. I remember particularly one fellow who claimed inability to carry such a heavy load. He was allowed to carry back separate arms, legs, and heads found strewn about. We walked to the railroad track to find the worst. Here some 60 had been put to digging their own graves with spoons and dishes. For some reason the detail was interrupted. Most of these were violently murdered, chopped to pieces; the axe was still there.

As we drove from the camp we saw more horrible sights. Some other prisoners had escaped. Either the injections had not taken effect on them or else in the rush they had been skipped. Some were lying dead several miles away. Some were walking – walking death. They could barely move their legs and were stooped almost double. One particular fellow I'm never going to forget. I haven't seen a better soldier. He heard our peep coming a long time before we got to him. With the most painful effort he turned toward us, brought himself to attention, and saluted. The effort he used to do that was more, far more, than he could spare.

Note: the above comments of Robert J. Hartwig were made when the 12th Armored Division liberated the Landsburg Concentration Camp in the spring of 1945. This particular camp, prior to being a concentration death camp, was a prison where Hitler had been held in 1924 and, again, was also where Hitler wrote Mein Kampf. The comments and the accompanying pictures in Appendix B show in detail the horrible conditions experienced in the concentration and extermination camps operated in Germany during World War II.

APPENDIX B

Photographs of the Landsburg Concentration Camp after Liberating the Concentration Camp

Taken by Robert J. Hartwig
C Company, 134th Ordinance Battalion,
12th Armored Division

Long piles of dead awaiting burial. It was a barren and cold place, cold in the mind's way. Death was too common.

They were thin dead, starved dead. Open sores and some burned black.

There were many. There were striped prisoner suits.

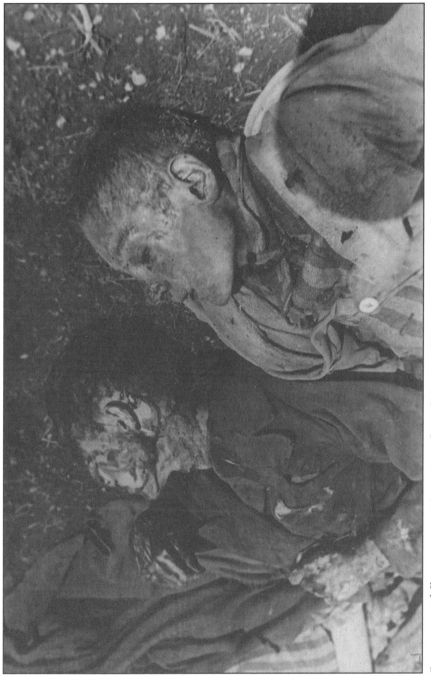

Some young fellows were not in a starved condition yet. They were beaten to death.

The oxygen the treatment is easy to find. They just ran out of air. Often it took a long time for them to die. The stragglers were beat or shot as they lay.

Beaten—shot—thin—young, and what the Nazis did not want to live.

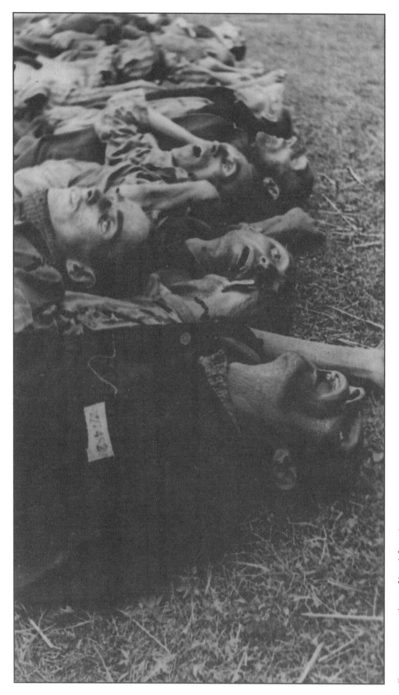

Some were given liquid poison.

Thin—no air.

Young eyes open—what will we do about it.

An old man. He suffered.

Mighty little meat one had on his bones. Tight waxy skin. Many were naked.

Some more shriveled up. Shrunk is maybe a better word. Naked and burned.

Some were old

Civilians were paired off and marched to the outer areas to pick more dead.

Captain Jones—out by the railroad.

Two carried one dead.

Some huts were doused with gasoline and fired while the prisoners were still alive.

Huts were low, filthy, meanly constructed affairs. Floors were below ground level. Note shelves along the edge for sleeping.

Some decapitated, all in this pile were chopped up in some manner.

This fellow has his arm chopped off at the elbow, his left arm.

Some burned.

The Nazis dug mass graves.

Thin—naked—open sores.

This fellow was chopped almost in two, through his stomach. Note the facial expression.

The dead SS Guard—his big, fat body among the emaciated corpses. The dead.

Can't be enough breath.

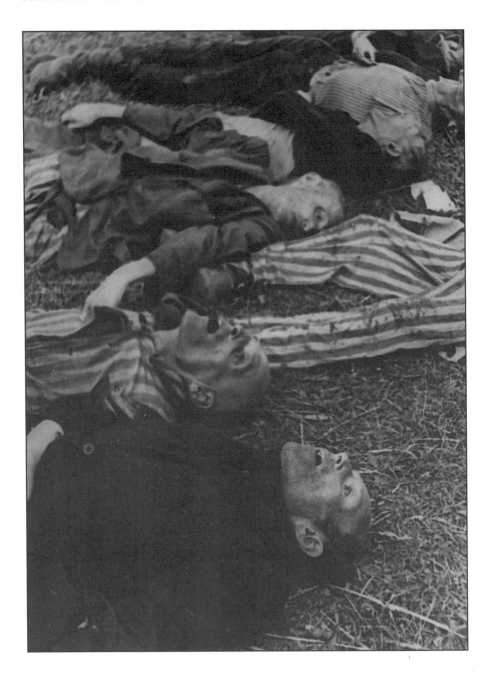

APPENDIX C

"To All Prisoners of War! The Escape from Prison Camps Is No Longer a Sport!"

G ermany has always kept to the Hague Convention and only punished recaptured prisoners of war with minor disciplinary punishment. Germany will still maintain these principles of International Law. But England has besides fighting at the front in an honest manner instituted an illegal warfare in non-combat zones in the form of gangster commandos, terror bandits, and sabotage troops even up to the frontiers of Germany.

They say in a captured secret and confidential English Military Pamphlet, *The Handbook of Modern Irregular Warfare*, "The days when we could practice the rules of sportsmanship are over. For the time being, every soldier must be a potential gangster and must be prepared to adopt their methods whenever necessary.

"The sphere of operations should always include the enemy's own country, any occupied territory, and in certain circumstances, such neutral countries as he is using as a source of supply."

England has with these instructions opened up a non-military form of gangster war!

Germany is determined to safeguard her homeland, and especially her war industry and provisional centers for the fighting fronts. Therefore it has become necessary to create strictly forbidden zones, called death zones, in which all unauthorized trespassers will be immediately shot on sight.

Escaping prisoners of war, entering such death zones, will certainly lose their lives. They are therefore in constant danger for being mistaken for enemy agents or sabotage groups.

Urgent warning is given against making future escapes!

In plain English: stay in the camp where you will be safe! Breaking out of it is now a damned dangerous act.

The chances of preserving your life are almost nil!

All police and military guards have been given the most strict orders to shoot on sight all suspected persons.

Escaping from prison camps has ceased to be a sport!

APPENDIX D

Soldiers of the British Commonwealth!

Soldiers of the United States of America!

The great Bolshevik offensive has now crossed the frontiers of Germany. The men in the Moscow Kremlin believe the way is open for the conquest of the Western World. This will certainly be the decisive battle for us. But it will also be the decisive battle for England, for the United States, and for the maintenance of Western Civilization.

Or whatever today remains of it.

The events in the Baltic States, in Poland, Hungary, and Greece, are proof enough for us all to see the real program behind the mask of Moscow's so-called "limited national aims" and reveals to us how Moscow interprets democratic principles both for the countries she has conquered and also for Germany and for your countries as well.

It is also clear enough *today* that the issue at stake is not merely the destruction of Germany and the extermination of the German race. *The fate of your country too is at stake.* This means the fate of your wives, of your children, and your home. It also means everything that makes life livable, loveable, and honorable for you.

Each one of you who has watched the development of Bolshevism throughout this war knows in his innermost heart the truth about Bolshevism. Therefore we are now addressing you as white men to other white men. This is not an appeal. At least we feel there is no alternative for any of us, who feels himself a citizen of our continent and our civilization, to not stop the red flood here and now.

Extraordinary events demand extraordinary measures and decisions. One of these decisions is now put up to you. We address ourselves to you regardless of your rank or of your nationality.

Soldiers! We are sure there are some amongst you who have recognized the danger of Bolshevik/Communism for his own country. We are sure that many of you have seen clearly what this war is now leading to. We are sure that many of you see what the consequences of the destruction of Europe – not just of Germany but of Europe – will mean to your own country. Therefore we want to make the following proposal to all of you:

We think that our fight has also become your fight. If there are some amongst you who are willing to take the consequences and who are willing to join the ranks of the German soldiers who fight in this battle that will decide both the fate of Germany and the fate of your countries, we should like to know it. We invite you to join our ranks and the tens of thousands of volunteers from the communist crushed and conquered nations of Eastern Europe, which have had to choose between submission under a most brutal Asiatic rule or a national existence in the future under European ideas, many of which, of course, are your own ideas.

Whether you are willing to fight in the front line or in the service corps we make you this solemn promise: whoever as a soldier of his own nation is willing to join the common front for the common cause, will be freed immediately after the victory of this present offensive and can return to his own country via Switzerland.

All that we have to ask from you is the word of the gentlemen not to fight directly or indirectly for the cause of Bolshevik/Communism so long as this war continues.

At this moment we do not ask you to think about Germany. We ask you to think about your own country, we ask you just to measure the chances which you and your people at home would have to do in case the Bolshevik/Communism onslaught should overpower Europe. We must and we will put an end to Bolshevism and we will achieve this under all circumstances. Please inform the convey officer of your decision and you will receive the privileges of our own men for we expect you to share their duty. This is something that surpasses all national boundaries. The world today is confronted by the fight of the east against the west. We ask you to think it over.

Are you for the culture of the west or the barbaric Asiatic east?
Make your decision now!

APPENDIX E

German Orders, Office of the Commanding General Army Service Forces

The German prisoner of war regulations translated in this volume were located by a member of the provost marshal general's office shortly after the termination of hostilities in Europe. They have been translated and issued through the efforts of the liaison and research branch of the American Prisoners of War Information Bureau.

B. M. Bryan
Brigadier General
The Provost Marshal General

Note: inconsistencies exist both in numerical compilation form and in content in the translation of the German Orders into English through the efforts of the liaison and research branch of the American Prisoners of War Information Bureau. The complete document is not included herein, but consists mainly of those German Orders that are most significant with respect to Alien Prisoners of War held by the Germans.

Abbreviations of German Military Terms

Abbreviations	Translation
Abw	Counter intelligence
Ag.E.H.	Section for Replacement Training and Army Matters
AHA	General Army Office
Arb. Ndo.	Work detail
AWA	Section for General Armed Forces Armed Forces Matters
B.d.E.	Commander of the Replacement Training Army
Bkl.	Clothing
Ch.H.Ruest	Chief of Army Equipment
Dulag	Transit camp for prisoners of war
Gen.D.Pi	General of the engineers
Gen.Qu.	Quartermaster General
Genst.D.H.	Army General Staff
GVF	Fit for garrison duty in the field
GVH	Fit for garrison duty in the interior
H.D.St.O.	Army Disciplinary Regulations
H.D.V.	Army Service Regulations
H.P.A.	Army Personnel Office
HV	Army Administration
H.V.Bl.	Army bulletin
In.Fest.	Inspector of fortresses
Kriegsgef.	Prisoner of War Department
Kv.	Fit for war service
Oflag	Officer's prisoner of war camp
Ob.d.L.	Commander-in-Chief of the Air Force
O.K.H.	Army Supreme Command
O.K.M.	Navy Supreme Command
O.K.W.	Supreme Command of the Wehrmacht (Armed Forces)
P.A.	Personnel Office
P.U.	Mail censorship
R.d.L.	Reich Minister of Aviation
S.D.	Security Service
S.S.	Elite Guard of the National Socialist Party
Stalag	PW camp for enlisted men
VA	Army Administration Office
VO	Decree
Wam.	Guard detail
W.A.St.	Information Bureau for the Wehrmacht
W.F.St.	Armed Forces Operations Staff
W.Pr.	Wehrmacht Propaganda
W.V.	Army administration

120

Supreme Command of the Wehrmacht
Berlin-Schoeneber, 16 June 1941

Chief Group

1. **Prisoners of war of alien nationalities in enemy armies.** Frequently recurring doubts in determining the nationality of alien prisoners of war are not definitely resolved in that the **uniform** is the determining outward factor in establishing the fact of the prisoner's belonging to the respective armed forces. Accordingly, Polish prisoners of war captured in French uniforms will be considered **Frenchmen**, while Poles captured in Polish uniforms will be considered **Poles**.

2. **The title "camp officer" instead of "camp leader."** The title "camp leader" is not accepted in any of the regulations. It is therefore no longer to be used, and is to be replaced by: "first camp officer" and "second camp officer."

3. **Reward for the recapture of escaped prisoners of war.** The OKW has requested the German newspapers to publish the following:

   In view of the increase in the number of escape attempts by prisoners of war commonly occurring in the spring, the military and police service will welcome the cooperation of the general public. Persons offering effective aid in apprehending escaped prisoners of war may be granted financial awards, applications for which must be directed to the respective prisoner of war camp.

   The rewards herewith provided for are to be paid out of Reich funds…The reward of one individual shall not exceed 30 marks even when several prisoners of war are apprehended. The amount is fixed by the Commander of Prisoners of War having jurisdiction of the respective prisoner of war camp.

Group 1. Prisoners of War of Alien Nationalities In Enemy Armies.

4. **Personal contact of prisoners of war with women.**

   Certain inquires addressed to the OKW make it necessary to point out the following:

   The prohibition of 10 Jan. 1940 applies to association of prisoners of war with German women.

   It is therefore not necessary to submit a detailed report in cases of illicit traffic of prisoners with women of foreign nationality, unless certain circumstances make it a penal offense (rape, intercourse with minors, etc.).

   The question as to the prisoner's liability to disciplinary punishment is left to the discretion of the disciplinary superior officer. The inquiry of the Army District Command V of 29 April 1941 1 3330 is thereby settled.

5. **Questionnaires for French Officers.**

   The French Armistice Commission had some time ago requested, in connection with the reconstitution of the French Army, that newly arrived French prisoner of war officers in all the camps fill out questionnaires. Since the work is now finished, the questionnaires need not be filled out any longer.

6. **Transfers to officers' camp IV C Colditz.**

   Several officers' camps frequently transfer to officers' camp IV C prisoner of war officers who have not yet completed disciplinary sentences pending against them.

   As the few guardhouse cells in officers' camp IV C are currently occupied by prisoner of war officers serving sentences by the headquarters of the camp, the transfer of officer's camp IV C may be undertaken only after they have completed their previously imposed disciplinary sentences.

7. **Jews in the French Army.**

   A transfer of the Jews to special camps is not intended; **they must, however, be separated from the other prisoners of war** and, in case of enlisted men, must be assigned to work in closed groups outside the camp.

   Jews are not to be specially marked.

8. **Punishment of prisoners of war by the suspension of mail service.**

   Several cases have been recently reported where camp commandants have suspended prisoners of war mail service as a disciplinary measure.

   Attention is called to Art. 36, Sec. 1 of the Geneva Convention of 1929 prohibiting the stoppage or confiscation of incoming or outgoing mail of prisoners of war.

   Article 57, Sec. 2 merely provides that packages and money orders addressed to prisoners of war undergoing disciplinary punishment may be handed to them only after the completion of their sentence.

   The decision as to whether mail is to be handed out to prisoners of war under a court sentence rests with the competent penal authorities…

Supreme Command of the Wehrmacht
Berlin-Schoeneberg, 23 July 1941

3. **English books for training in radio broadcasting to foreign lands. (Talk work.)**

   In camps occupied by British prisoners of war several copies of the books named below will probably be found in possession of the prisoners:

Field Service Regulations, Vols. 1 & 2, Cavalry Training, Manual of Organization and Administration, Artillery Training, Field Service Pocket Book, Infantry Section Training, Infantry Training Vols. 1 & 2, Engineer Training.

It is requested that one copy of these books be procured and forwarded **directly** to the OKW/W Pr (IV hi) Berlin W 35, Bendlerstr. 10. Should other books of similar nature not mentioned above be found, it is requested that one copy of these, too, be forwarded. No statement as to where the books are being sent is to be made to the prisoners of war.

14. **Questionnaires on cases of death of prisoners of war.**

In the case of the death of a prisoner of war, in addition to the report to the Information Bureau of the Wehrmacht, a special questionnaire must be immediately filled out and submitted to the German Red Cross, Berlin SW 61 Bluecherplatz 2, so that the relatives of the deceased can be notified without delay (OKW file 2 F 24. 62a. Kriegsgef. Vi No. 135/11 dated 7 Jan 1941). **Direct** notification of the next of kin of the deceased is not permitted. **Double reports** are to be avoided. Should the prisoner of war die while in a hospital, the camp is to be informed of the date on which the questionnaire has been forwarded to the German Red Cross. No questionnaires are to be filled out in cases of death of **Russian** prisoners of war.

Supreme Command of the Wehrmacht
Berlin-Schoeneberg, 1 Sept. 1941

4. **Religious functions at prisoner of war camps.**

In view of the general lack of interpreters, it will be sufficient for a specially selected, qualified guard to be present at divine services in which only the **Sacrifice of the Mass is performed and Communion** is given, in order to see to it that the minister does not add anything in the way of a special sermon.

11. **Guard personnel in officers' camps.**

Complaints have been repeatedly made that guards, who are entirely unfit for their task by reason of physical disabilities (club foot, impaired hearing, marked near-sightedness, etc.) or low intelligence, are being used for the surveillance of prisoner of war officers.

For the sake of the prestige of the German Wehrmacht, officers' camps are to use only such personnel as are physically and mentally unobjectionable and who are thus not liable to produce an unfavorable impression on the prisoner of war officers. An appropriate exchange of personnel within the guard battalions is to be undertaken immediately.

Supreme Command of the Wehrmacht
Berlin-Schoeneberg, 8 Dec. 1941

14. **Supplying camp canteens with rubber collars for Yugoslav prisoner of war officers.**

The firm "Rheinische Gurmmi & Celluloid Fabrick," Mannheim, was exporting before the war considerable quantities of rubber collars to Yugoslavia, for use by officers of the Yugoslav army. The firm still has on hand about 700 dozen collars, left from an order which could not more be delivered and otherwise disposed of. The Chamber of Industry & Commerce in Mannheim has approached the OKW with the request to be permitted to sell the collars to canteens of those camps where Yugoslav prisoners of war officers are interned.

Since the disposal of these collars, usable only by Yugoslav officers, is in the interest of our national economy, the prisoner of war camps in question are being informed of the opportunity to purchase rubber collars from the firm Rheinische Gurmmi and Cellulois Fabrik Mannheim.

Supreme Command of the Wehrmacht

Prisoner of War Department
Berlin-Schoeneberg,
31 Dec. 1941, Badenschestr. 51

7. **Re: Tin Boxes of British Fliers.**

British fliers brought down have been found to carry with them tin cans containing a small saw made of steel, a map of northern France and the north German coast, chocolate, and concentrated food tablets. These tin cans presumably are to help the Britishers to avoid capture or to escape from imprisonment after capture. Such special equipment has been repeatedly found on British fliers. It apparently belongs to the "iron rations" (emergency kits) of the British air force.

Special attention is to be paid to this when capturing British fliers shot down or delivering them to a prisoner of war camp.

8. **Re: Informing newly arrived prisoners of war of camp regulations.**

There are cases on record where prisoners of war, newly arrived in a collecting camp **to be released**, and unfamiliar with the regulations of the new camp, were severely wounded or killed by warning shots.

Since the same regulations governing order and discipline in camps do not apply in all camps, care must be taken that newly arrived prisoners of war be immediately made familiar with the new regulations, even if their stay at the camp is to be temporary. Posting alone on blackboards and in the halls is not sufficient. A reliable prisoner of war non-commissioned officer or the camp spokesman may be entrusted with this task.

Supreme Command of the Wehrmacht
Chief of the Prisoner of War Department
Berlin-Schoeneberg
11 March 1942, Badensehestr. 51

5. **Re: Marking of Jews.**

The Jews in Germany are specially marked with a star, as a measure of the German government to identify them in the street, stores, etc. Jewish prisoners of war are not marked with a star, yet they have to be kept apart from the other prisoners of war as far as possible.

23. **Re: Cases of death of prisoners of war.**

Reports to the information Bureau of the Wehrmacht on deaths of prisoners of war and the corresponding notices to the German Red Cross through questionnaires are to be drawn up in such a way as to obviate the necessity of further time-consuming inquires.

The following is therefore to be observed:

1. The report of the death of a prisoner of war to the information Bureau of the Wehrmacht must indicate the **cause** of death in exact accordance with the facts, and also give the **place** of death in a way to make the competent registrar's office easily identifiable. It is not enough, for instance, to state: "Shot." Rather it must be worded: "Shot while trying to escape," or "Shot in the execution of a sentence." It is likewise not enough to give as place of death merely "Camp Erlensbusch," but rather "Camp Erlensbusch near village X." The exact location of a work detail in a death report is essential even when such detail is located near a *stalag*, as it cannot be automatically assumed that the two places belong to the same registrar district.

2. The report on the death of a prisoner of war to the Presidency of the German Red Cross constitutes the basis for

the notification of the family of the deceased. The death notice is prepared by the German Red Cross and is transmitted to the next of kin through the local Red Cross office of the latter. **The questionnaire proper** is then forwarded by the German Red Cross to the International Red Cross in Geneva.

In preparing the "death notice questionnaire," the following is to be observed:

a. The questionnaire must be speedily & fully filled out and promptly forwarded to the Presidency of the German Red Cross, Berlin S W 61Bluecherplatz 2. Only this agency is competent to receive such questionnaires. Sending same to any other agency is not permitted, even though the questionnaire was made up by the International Red Cross in Geneva.

b. Careful formulation of the cause of death in case of unnatural death, as the questionnaire is to be sent abroad (International Red Cross).

c. The nationality of the deceased must be given right after the name and the name of the country after the address of his next-of-kin.

d. The last question must be answered in the greatest detail, insofar as there are no objections to the answer becoming known abroad.

3. For the time being no questionnaire is to be filled out for deceased **Soviet prisoners of war**.

4. Deaths of prisoners of war are not to be reported to the Protecting Powers either by camp commandants, or by the spokesman.

75. **Re: Contact between French & Soviet prisoners of war.**

Soviet prisoners of war must be strictly kept apart from prisoners of other nationalities, particularly Frenchmen. They should also be permitted no opportunity for establishing such contacts at their place of work.

Strictest measures are to be taken against contractors who fail to comply with the above security requirements.

79. **Re: Position of prisoners of war officers with respect to German personnel.**

A particular incident has moved the Fuhrer to emphasize anew that, when considering the relationship between prisoner of war officers and German camp personnel, the most humble German national is deemed more important that the highest ranking subject of an enemy power.

111. **Re: Prisoners of war as blood donors.**

"For reasons of race hygiene, prisoners of war are not acceptable as blood donors for members of the German community, since the possibility of a prisoner of war of Jewish origin being used as a donor cannot be excluded with certainty."

171. **Re: Display of flags in prisoner of war quarters.**

Since the British government has forbidden the display of German flags in prisoner of war quarters, **British** flags are to be immediately withdrawn in all German camps. The prisoners are to be notified of the above reason during the roll call.

176. **Re: Reparation for willful destruction.**

Prisoners of war proven guilty of willfully destroying or damaging state or other property as, for instance, in connection with tunnel construction, are to be punished and, in addition, made liable for damages. Should the actual perpetrators not be discovered, and should the prisoners of war involved be British, the whole camp community may be collectively held responsible for damage – which is the customary practice in England & Canada (Canteen funds).

199. **Re: Handling of tin cans for prisoners of war.**

In a few camps it has lately become common practice, when issuing tin cans to prisoners of war, to be satisfied with the opening of the cans and a superficial examination of their contents, and then to hand the open can and contents to the prisoners. When underway, even unopened cans are issued as marching rations. It is again pointed out that, for reasons of security, only the contents of the tin can may be issued to the prisoner of war. Deviation from this rule may be permitted only in exceptional cases, as when other receptacles are not available. In such cases the tin cans themselves must be examined as a security measure prior to their issuance.

223. **Re: Shooting & severe wounding of prisoners of war & civilian internees (except Poles, Serbs, and Soviet Russians).**

1. An inquiry by a court officer or any other qualified officer is to be initiated in each case of fatal shooting or wounding of a British, French, Belgian, or American prisoner of war or civilian internee. If comrades of the prisoner of war or civilian internee were witnesses of the incident, they, too, will be heard. The result of the inquiry and a copy of the examination proceedings are to be submitted immediately to the OKW Kriegsgef. Allg. (la), reference being made to the file number below. This report is to be designated as "Report on the use of arms by soldier X." A detailed report against soldier X will be necessary only when there is suspicion of the latter having committed a legally punishable act and when an immediate court decision appears desirable.

2. Re: Casualties of British, French, Belgian, and American prisoners of war resulting from enemy air raids.

Deaths & injuries of British, French, Belgian, and American prisoners of war resulting from enemy air raids are to be reported in writing immediately after the raid to the OKW/Kriegsgef. Allg. (V), giving the file number below. The following are to be stated in the report:

1. First name and surname
2. Rank
3. Prisoner of war number
4. Date of birth
5. Wounded or dead
6. Address of next of kin

In addition, the camp headquarters are to send carbon copies of the reports directly to: the Bureau Scapini, Berlin W35 Standarten Strasse 12, when French prisoners of war are involved, and to the Belgian Prisoner of War Committee, Berlin W 8, Hotel Adlon, Unter den Linden, when Belgian prisoners are involved.

A report is also to be submitted to the Information Bureau of the Wehrmacht.

239. Re: Transport of recaptured or unreliable prisoners of war.

A certain case where a guard was murdered by four recaptured Soviet prisoners of war during transport after dark makes it appropriate to point out that recaptured prisoners of war or prisoners known to be unreliable should, as far as possible, not be transported after nightfall. Should the transport after dark be unavoidable, at least two guards must be assigned to the detail.

246. Re: Securing prisoner of war camps against escape attempts.

1. **Fencing in of the camp.**

   The wire entanglements between the inner and outer fences must be so constructed that an escaping prisoner of war will be able neither to climb over them, nor to crawl under them. Anchor posts should just only slightly be out of the ground.

2. **The foreground of the stockade**, as well as the space between the warning wire and the fence, must present an open field of view and of fire. It is therefore to be kept free of brushwood and all other objects impeding vision.

3. **Watch Towers.**

There are no generally applicable detailed instructions for the construction of watchtowers. It depends on the topographic and climatic conditions of the camp and must provide the best possible field of view and of fire.

272. **Re: Procuring wrapping paper for Soviet corpses.**

The camp headquarters will henceforth report the amount of oil paper, tarpaper, and asphalt paper needed for the burial of dead Soviet prisoners of war directly to the nearest paper wholesaler. The latter will then apply to the competent Army Raw Material Board for an army paper ration certificate. The further procedure is familiar to the wholesalers.

In view of the scarcity of the above kinds of paper, they may be used only for wrapping corpses. Their use is to be to the barest minimum.

278. **Re: Internment of fallen or deceased members of the enemy armed forces.**

To remove any doubt as to whether prisoners of war shot during flight or in acts of insubordination are entitled to burial with military honors, the following is ordered:

1. As a matter of principle, every honorably fallen enemy is to be buried with military honors.

2. Flight is not dishonorable, unless dishonorable acts were committed during such flight.

3. Cases of insubordination must be individually examined as to whether acts reflecting on the soldiers' honor have been

committed. Where such violations of the soldiers' code of honor have been established without question, military honors during burial are to be excluded.

279. **Re: Accepting bribes by guards.**

A private first class on guard duty in a certain camp has on several occasions accepted bribes of cigarettes and chocolate from prisoners of war and permitted them to escape without interference, instead of reporting them to his superior at their very first suggestion. He was sentenced to death for dereliction of guard duty, for willfully releasing prisoners of war, and for accepting bribes.

All guard personnel entrusted with the custody of prisoners of war are to be informed of the above with the appropriate comments. The announcement is to be repeated at least every three months.

313. **Re: Death sentence of a prisoner of war guard member of a regional defense unit.**

The private first class Jungmichel, assigned to a guard detail at an officers' prisoner of war camp, entered into relations with a Polish officer interned at that camp. He supplied the officer, at the latter's request, with various tools, maps, and other items intended to facilitate the escape of this and other prisoners of war. Jungmichel was sentenced to death by the Reich Court Martial for war treason. The sentence was carried out on 5 March 1943.

The above sentence is to be made known to all the members of the administration headquarters and the guard units.

324. **Re: Use of identification tags by prisoners of war.**

To prepare and to conceal escapes, more and more prisoners of war use the device of exchanging identification tags with other prisoners, or of getting rid of them altogether. Such practices are to be prevented by the imposition of heavy penalties, if necessary.

When calling the roll, a check of the identification tags must not be neglected.

404. **Re: Preventing escape by taking away trousers and boots.**

When establishing new work details, an appropriate room is to be set aside for the safe storage of trousers and boots taken from the prisoners of war for the night.

422. **Re: Thefts from bomb-wrecked homes.**

When prisoners of war are assigned to wreckage clearing jobs after air raids, their attention is again to be called to the death penalty as provided by the reference order.

504. **Re: Use of firearms against prisoners of war.**

The service regulations for prisoners of war affairs do not provide for any warning shots. Should the occasion for the use of firearms arise, they must be fired with the intent to hit.

619. **Re: Securing of prisoner of war transports against escape.**

The freight cars for the transport of prisoners of war frequently carry boards in the sliding doors, arranged so as to pass in stove pipes. These boards are to be removed before shipping the prisoners of war, since they render the barb wiring of the doors difficult and can easily be forced.

To better secure the sliding doors of these freight cars, not only the bolts, but also the door casters, may be wired.

679. **Re: Fixing of bayonets while guarding prisoners of war.**

It is in order to call attention to Sec. 475 of the Compilation of Orders 30 of 16 Oct. 1943, whereby guards are to stand with their rifles loaded and placed at "safe," and their bayonets fixed, unless the camp commandant, for special reasons, orders a deviation from that rule. This order is extended to provide that guard details accompanying prisoner of war transports or on their way from and to work have their bayonets fixed. French bayonets, which are too long, can be ground down to the standard size of German bayonets.

687. Re: Private conversation between German soldiers and prisoners of war.

All conversations between German soldiers and prisoners of war not justified by the needs of the service or the work assignment are forbidden.

It is the primary responsibility of the company commanders to educate their subordinates to the importance of maintaining the proper distance between themselves and the prisoners of war and to put a stop to all attempts of the prisoners to start unauthorized conversations.

692. Re: Assault on guards.

Lately several guards have been attacked and killed while transferring prisoners of war after dark.

Prisoners of war are to be moved on foot after dark only in cases of utmost necessity, and only under particularly vigilant surveillance.

Attention is to be directed continually to this prohibition and to the danger of attack.

714. Re: Taking away boots and trousers from prisoners of war in work details.

In order to render more difficult the escape of prisoners of war assigned to and quartered in work details, their boots and trousers are generally to be taken away for the night and stored in such a manner as to make their recovery by the prisoners impossible.

715. **Re: Air defense measures in the prisoner of war service.**

During an air raid alarm prisoners of war may be assigned to the defense of their own quarters and workshops in exactly the same manner as the German employees.

After the all-clear signal they may also be assigned to damage control work in other places, but, in this case, must be kept under safe, regular surveillance.

718. **Re: Behavior of prisoners of war during air raids.**

1. Guarding of Prisoner of War Labor Commandos.

   In workshops that, according to the air defense regulations, must be vacated by their crews during air raids, provisions must be made, in agreement with the shop management, that the prisoners of war be kept at all times under surveillance by the guards and latter's assistants while leaving the premises and remaining outside of same, as well as while returning thereto. Alarm plans are to be prepared fixing the place of the air raid shelters and the ways of reaching same.

2. Marching Prisoners of War Seeking Protection in Public and Private Air Raid Shelters.

   No objection may be raised against prisoners of war on march seeking protection in public air raid shelters in a sudden air attack; private shelters, too, may be used by prisoners of war in an emergency, provided the number of the prisoners is small.

   It is presumed that the German civilian population will take precedence and that the prisoners of war will be kept close together in one room or one place. Dispersal among the civilian population is forbidden. In case of need, the prisoners of war may be distributed under guard in smaller groups in several parts of the air raid shelter.

743. **Re: Working together of prisoners of war and concentration camp internees.**

The working together of prisoners of war and concentration camp internees has repeatedly led to difficulties and has unfavorably affected the efficiency of the prisoners of war. Employment of prisoners of war and of concentration camp internees on the same job at the same time is therefore forbidden. They may be employed in the same shop only when complete separation is assured.

837. **Re: Verification of personal data supplied by escaped and recaptured prisoners of war.**

Recaptured prisoners of war often falsely give to the camp authorities, to whom they have been delivered, names and identification numbers of other prisoners of war of their former camp and of the same nationality, known to them as having likewise escaped. Now and then they try to hide behind the name and the identification number of prisoners of war whose approximate description and circumstances of whose escape they had learned at the very time of their own escape. Such attempts at camouflage are made particularly by escaped and recaptured prisoners of war having a court suit pending against them at their former camp.

Security officers of prisoner of war camps are to verify in each case the personal data supplied by recaptured prisoners of war from other camps.

838. **Re: Death penalty for prisoners of war for illicit intercourse with German women.**

The Serbian prisoner of war, Pvt. Pentalija Kabanica, identification number 104325YB, was sentenced to death by a court martial for the military offense consisting of illicit traffic with a German woman, combined with rape. He had rendered defenseless the peasant women in whose farm he was engaged as a laborer, and then used her sexually. The sentence is to be made known in this version to all the prisoners of war.

840. **Re: Killings & serious injuries of prisoners of war and civilian internees (except Poles, Serbs, and Russians).**

The reference order has often not been observed, with the result that the OKW has had again and again to learn of cases of violent deaths of prisoners of war through the Ministry of Foreign Affairs or the Protecting Powers. This situation is unbearable in view of the reciprocity agreement with the enemy governments. The following additional orders are therefore announced herewith:

To 1. Every case of violent death or serious injury is to be promptly reported through channels to the OKW/Kriegsgef. Allg. (lib) (for exception see 2). In cases involving the use of arms, written depositions of the participants and witnesses, including prisoners of war, are to be attached; action is to be taken by the camp commandant and the prisoner of war commander ("Commandeur").

The name, camp, identification number, and home address of the prisoner of war involved must be given. Should a long search for these be necessary, a preliminary report is to be submitted at once, and the result of the search reported later.

Reports are also necessary, in addition to cases involving the use of arms, in cases of **accidents of all kinds**, of suicides, etc.; written depositions of witnesses will be mostly unnecessary here.

To 2. Losses due to enemy action are to be reported immediately to the OKW/Kriegsgef. Alllg.)V) in the form prescribed by reference order 2.

848. **Re: Rendering prisoner of war camps recognizable.**

Prisoner of war camps in the home war zone are not to be made recognizable for enemy air forces.

853. **Re: Prisoners of war mustered into Waffen SS (volunteer groups).**

Prisoners of war who have voluntarily reported for service in the Waffen SS have had their lives threatened by their fellow prisoners of war for their friendliness to Germany and their willingness to serve.

Representatives of the main SS office engaged in recruiting prisoners of war for the Waffen SS in the prisoner of war camps are to be reminded by the camp commandants that the security of these prisoners of war requires that steps be taken to have them speedily removed.

Should the enlisted prisoners of war not be able to take their physical examination at the SS, the representatives of the main SS Bureau must, when taking the prisoners away, report those turned back to the original camp in order that they may be assigned to another camp.

876. **Re: Treatment of Jewish prisoners of war.**

Ref: 1. Compilation of Orders No. 1 of 16 June 1941, Sec. 7.
2. Compilation of Orders No. 11 of 11 March 1942, Sec. 5.

The combined above reference orders provide as follows:

1. The bringing together of Jewish prisoners of war in separate camps is not intended; on the other hand, all Jewish prisoners of war are to be kept separated from the other prisoners of war in *stalags*, and officers' camps, and – in the case of enlisted personnel – to be grouped in closed units for work outside the camp. Contact with the German population is to be avoided.

   Special marking of the clothing of Jewish prisoners of war is not necessary.

2. In all other respects Jewish prisoners of war are to be treated like the other prisoners of war belonging to the respective

armed forces (with respect to work duty, protected personnel, etc.).

3. Jewish prisoners of war who had lost their citizenship by
   Regulation 11 of the Reich Citizenship Law of 25 Nov. 1941
   (R.G.B.I. 1941 1 p. 722), are to be buried – in case they die
   in captivity – without the usual military honors.

894. **Re: Reports on escapes of prisoners of war.**

Mass escapes, escapes of small groups, or single officers – from
the colonel upward – as well as of prominent personalities rep-
resented such a menace to security as to render the disciplinary
handling of the matter in accordance with paragraph 16a K St
Vo entirely inadequate, in view of the possible consequences of
such escapes. Detailed reports must under all circumstances be
submitted concerning the activity of the custodial agencies that
made such serious flights possible, whether through dereliction
of duty or through mere carelessness.

895. **Re: Strict house arrest and preliminary (investigation) arrest of
prisoners of war, including prisoner of war officers.**

A concrete case makes it appropriate to point out the following:

1. An increase in rations through delivery of food and other
   articles of consumption by all outsiders, including the International Red Cross, is absolutely forbidden.

2. Additional food and other articles of consumption may be
   obtained by prisoner of war officers only through purchase,
   contingent upon good behavior, and in moderate quantities.
   In each individual case the approval of the camp commandant is necessary.

3. Tobacco may be obtained in quantity within the general
   limits provided in the smoker's care, but only when the
   danger of fire or disturbance of discipline is absent.

Note to 1-3: Prisoners of war under preliminary arrest, in order to obtain additional items of food and of general consumption, must also secure the consent of the investigation officer (leader) or the state attorney.

897. **Re: Escapes during transport.**

There is reason to point out that prisoners of war during transport sometimes try to use the toilet for escape. The guards must therefore, as a rule, accompany the prisoner of war to the toilet on transports and must keep their eyes on him with the door open. Should the prisoner of war close the toilet door with the intention to escape, the guard must fire on him through the door without warning.

APPENDIX F

Map of Concentration Camps "Reich 1942"

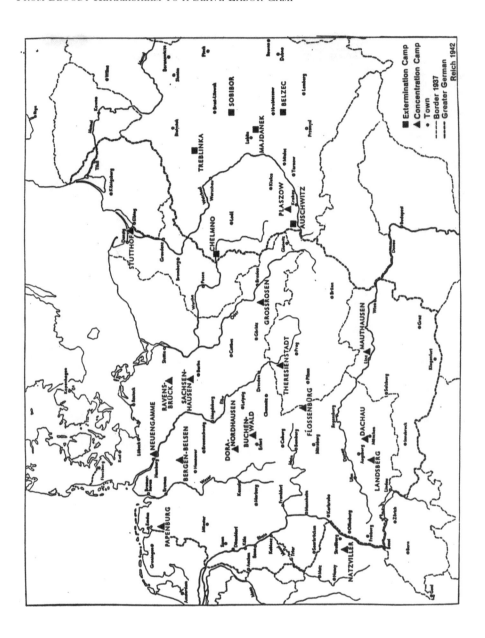

APPENDIX G

James E. Muschell
World War II
Service Medals

James E. Muschell served in World War II in Co. B, 43rd Tank Battalion, 12th armored Division. The following are medals he received.

From the United States of America:

Two Purple Hearts
European Theater Medal with 3 Bronze Battle Stars for Central Europe, Ardennes-Alsace and the Rhineland
Good Conduct Medal
Prisoner of War Medal
American Defense Medal
Victory Medal

From the United Kingdom:

U.K. Prisoner of War Medal for being assigned to a labor camp with British, Russian, Polish and Jewish prisoners.

From the Republic of France:

French Croix De Guerre
Medaille Commemorative Francaise
Croix du Combattant Voluntaire
Liberation of Alsace for Cities: Mulhouse, Strasbourg, and Colmar
Croix du Combattant
Medaille France Libre
Croix du Lorraine

Member of:

American Ex-Prisoner of War Association
12th Armored Division Association
American Order of the French Croix De Guerre
Veterans of Foreign Wars
American Legion
Order of the Purple Heart
Disabled American Veterans

APPENDIX H

James E. Muschell Diplome, Republique Francaise Mercredi, 8 May 2002

References

1. "Overshadowed by the Bulge 'Nordwind.'" National Historian J. J. Witmeyer Jr. from *Purple Heart*, Vol. LXV, Number 3, May/June 2000.

2. *Nuremberg Diary* by G. M. Gilbert Ph.D., New American Library of World Literature, 1947. 501 Madison Avenue, New York, NY.

3. German Prisoner of War Regulations Section 743: Re: Working together of prisoners of war and concentration camp internees. The working together of prisoners of war and concentration camp internees has repeatedly led to difficulties and has unfavorably affected the efficiency of the prisoners of war. Employment of prisoners of war and of concentration camp internees on the same job at the same

time is therefore forbidden. They must be employed in the same shop only when complete separation is assured. "Ignored by the German High Command 1944-'45."

4. "The Hellcats 12th Armored Division, 1942-1945." Reprinted in 1978 by Battery Press, P.O. Box 3107, Uptown Station, Nashville, TN 37219.

5. "All told, after World War II, half a million Allied prisoners of war and displaced Europeans were swallowed up into Soviet-occupied territory, including an estimated 20,000 American prisoners of war and MIAs (Missing in Action). While 28,662 American POWs and MIAs in Germany were repatriated, many other MIAs and about 12,000 U.S. POWs in German camps liberated by the Red Army simply vanished. No U.S. POW of World War II has ever returned from the former USSR. A lack of honesty by the U.S. government left our nation with more than 78,000 missing from World War II." Reported by John M. G. Brown, POW/MIA expert for the Senate Select Committee on POW/MIA affairs. Published in *American Legion*, Sept. 1995.

6. Bejec Woichevski was a Polish fellow slave laborer detached from the nearby concentration camp Bergen Belsen. He also worked in the fuel refining plant in Hannover, Germany. I am unsure of the correct spelling of his name.

7. "*I Was There!*" by Lt. Col. M. William Mark, USAF (Retired), Forest Hills, N.Y. *Ex-POW Bulletin*, May 2000, p. 39.

8. "*Soldiers of Berga.*" Confirmation by Bernie Melnick of Cape Coral, Florida, *Ex-POW Bulletin*, April 1984, p. 27.

9. *American Ex-Prisoners of War Service Foundation*, Vol. 1, Issue 1, 2001.

10. *Ex-POW Bulletin*, Vol. 41, April 1984.

11. "Battle of the Bulge" by William K. Goolrick and Ogden Tanner, *World War II Time Life Books*, Alexandria, Virgina.

12. *Busting the Bulge* by David Cooley, VFW, Dec. 1994.

13. *Winter Storm* by Lise M. Pommois, p. 102

14. *Seven Days in January* by Wolf T. Zoepf, Adjutant, 3rd Battalion, SS-Mountain Infantry.

15. *Herrlisheim, Death of an American Combat Command* by David T. Zabecki and Keith Wooster. *World War II Magazine* Publication.

16. F. George Hatt Jr, Historian for 12th Armored Division Association, and Wilhelm Balbach, 10th SS Panzer Division.

17. Ibid., 16.

18. Admiral Karl Doenitz, who surrendered Germany unconditionally.

19. Ibid., 16.

20 Ibid., 16.

21 Ibid., 11.

22. Ibid., 4.

23. Ibid., 11.

24. Ibid., 11.

25. Ibid., 11.